Kitchen Design & Remodeling

Complete Handyman's Library™
Handyman Club of America
Minneapolis, Minnesota

Published in 1995 by
Handyman Club of America
12301 Whitewater Drive
Minnetonka, Minnesota 55343

Copyright © 1995 by Cy DeCosse Incorporated

Published by arrangement with Cy DeCosse Incorporated
ISBN 0-86573-749-5

Printed on American paper by
R. R. Donnelley & Sons Co.
99 98 97 96 / 5 4 3 2

CREDITS:
Created by: The Editors of Cy DeCosse Incorporated
and the staff of the Handyman Club of America
in cooperation with Black & Decker. **BLACK&DECKER®**
is a trademark of Black & Decker (US), Incorporated
and is used under license.

Handyman Club of America:
   Book Marketing Manager: Cal Franklin
   Book Marketing Coordinator: Jay McNaughton

Contents

Introduction

Remodeling your kitchen is one of the most desirable building projects. Turning an outdated, undersized or poorly laid out kitchen into a beautiful and functional highlight of your home is very rewarding: it increases your enjoyment of a room your family spends a great deal of time in, and increases the value of your house as well. *Kitchen Design & Remodeling* will show you everything you need to know to achieve such results for your home.

Careful planning will help you have a successful project. The first section, **What Makes a Great Kitchen,** shows you many successful kitchen design ideas to help you visualize the kitchen you desire. Once you evaluate the problems in your existing kitchen and determine the changes you wish to make, you can begin the practical planning of the actual building project. You see how to plan around your lifestyle needs and choose the materials, storage options, appliances and fixtures that will fit your needs. You also learn how to use color and lighting in your design scheme, as well as how to develop your own design style.

The rest of the book shows you how to work with countertops, flooring, cabinets, plumbing and appliances to make your design a reality. First you see how to make an effective floor plan for the project to ensure that your new kitchen will be as functional as it is beautiful. You also learn which tools you will need to perform the various project tasks.

Countertops teaches you everything you need to know about building and installing post-form, laminate, tile and solid-surface countertops. **Flooring** demonstrates how to remove old flooring, install the proper underlayment and work with the various types of flooring: wood and vinyl tiles, vinyl sheet goods, hardwood and ceramic floor tile. **Cabinets** shows you the options of painting or refacing your existing cabinets, or how to choose and install new cabinets. **Plumbing & Appliances** gives you the basics for sink, faucet and drain installations. It also shows how to install a food disposer, dishwasher or vent hood and make the simple gas and electrical hookups needed for other appliances.

Begin your kitchen remodeling project by looking through the many examples of gorgeous kitchens, and finish it by following the step-by-step illustrated instructions that show you how to make the kitchen of your dreams a reality.

A great kitchen is a culinary showplace offering easy care and convenience. A handsome, easy-to-clean butcher-block countertop helps the cook coordinate the activity in this busy country kitchen.

WHAT MAKES A GREAT KITCHEN?

A great kitchen is one created with your specific lifestyle in mind. It should be a comfortable, attractive and efficient place to work and socialize. Simply put, a great kitchen is a room your family loves.

To help you plan your great kitchen, we have assembled more than 100 color photographs of outstanding kitchen designs and features.

The first section shows how you can customize your kitchen to reflect your family's lifestyle and tastes. It highlights the elements of a great kitchen: interesting color schemes, unique building materials, creative lighting, space-expand-ing storage units, and well-placed appliances and fixtures.

The second section is filled with pictures of fantastic kitchens. Included are all the classic styles, ranging from traditional to country to contemporary. You see how to design with these styles while incorporating your family's lifestyle and tastes to create your own personal look.

Whether you are sprucing up your old kitchen, planning a major overhaul, or designing a completely new kitchen, these pictures are sure to give you plenty of useful ideas.

Storage. Pantry has adjustable wire baskets that will accommodate most containers. Swinging panels allow access to back shelves. For efficient storage, use vertical as well as horizontal space.

Focal point. Elegant brass range hood steals the show in this understated contemporary kitchen. Select one stunning feature, material or color, and make it the center of the kitchen plan.

Color. Buy a lot of style on a little budget. Accent a neutral scheme with bold, bright accessories, as in this white and red kitchen. A monochromatic color plan is soothing; high-contrast colors are lovely and energizing.

PLANNING

Fit your lifestyle

Planning a kitchen starts with a close look at your family. How large is it? Is it growing? Consider your family's eating and cooking habits. Who eats at home? How often? Does your family eat together? Where?

Keep in mind the processes of food preparation, from baking bread to basting a bird. Consider how much cooking is done each week. Is there more than one cook? Are fresh or prepared foods more important? How often is equipment like a griddle, a food processor or pasta maker used? The answers to these questions will help you select appliances and estimate the food and equipment storage space that will be needed.

Include socializing in this lifestyle inventory. Does your family enjoy entertaining? How often? Where? For how many guests? Is entertaining informal or formal? Do guests help with kitchen duties? A floor plan begins to emerge as you consider how the kitchen relates to the entertaining areas.

Also list special family needs, such as space for a laundry, a sewing and ironing area, a phone center, a hobby counter or seating for children.

A large table is the center of activity for a busy family kitchen. Here, a large kitchen table becomes a colorful party table for a child's birthday celebration.

Bright white countertops and flooring give this informal family kitchen a fresh, clean feel. For the family on the go, the convenient center island includes a cooktop with enough counter space around it to accommodate two diners.

Create an exciting focal point in your kitchen. Put a ceramic-tile mural in the spotlight, for example, or pine cabinets stenciled with a country motif. Play up an architectural feature in an older home; create interest in a simple contemporary setting by using an unusual material for countertops or cabinets.

If you choose this bold approach to kitchen design, make sure the focal point is planned carefully in terms of scale, shape, color and materials. Visualize the kitchen as a complementary setting for the highlighted feature.

Focus on shape. *Lively angles define this unusual kitchen. The island and light fixture repeat the shape of the triangular room. The practical benefit: space is used efficiently.*

Focus on a fireplace. *Floor-to-ceiling fireplace is the centerpiece of this contemporary kitchen. Details like a raised hearth, brick firebox, simple mantel and gleaming lamps enhance its appeal.*

Contemporary and country combine *in this clever kitchen design. The streamlined look of the cupboards and cabinets creates a smooth contemporary feel, while a country-style table with a butcher-block top is the centerpiece of this kitchen. The woven seats and old-style design of the chairs add a casual country accent that blends well with the contemporary design of the cabinets.*

By coordinating furnishings, accessories, colors and materials for any room, you can express your personal style. Usually this individual look reflects a classic style, such as stately traditional, casual country, sleek and simple contemporary or an eclectic mix of styles.

By studying the elements of classic styles in design books, store displays, design seminars and through consultations with kitchen planners, you can refine your planning skills. Careful planning is especially critical for those who are tackling a kitchen design project for the first time. Remember, function comes first in an active kitchen. Use simple treatments for cabinet fronts and countertops. Keep the flooring and window treatments simple as well.

Your goal is to create a kitchen that is a thing of beauty because it works so well, and also confidently expresses your personal style.

A classic black and white design scheme is created in a simple white kitchen by adding a striped awning and accenting with various black accessories. Clever choices of attractive accessories makes this kitchen fashionable as well as functional.

Distinctive double-arch cabinets dress up this cottage kitchen. Arched ceiling moldings repeat the cabinet pattern. Space expanding details; salmon and eggshell color scheme, drop-leaf rolling table stored under counter, and floor-to-ceiling cabinets.

Inspirational mix. Country/contemporary. Stark white kitchen is warmed with a wood ceiling, rustic antique dining table and American collectibles.

COLOR

Pulls a room together

A strong color scheme gives a kitchen character and unifies the design. Consider a monochromatic plan, in which one color, or shades of one color, dominates. Use this color on large areas, such as cabinets, counters or walls.

You can set a mood with color. Dark tones bring walls inward, creating intimate space; whites and neutrals open up a room. Warm up a north-facing kitchen with reds, yellows and oranges. Cool a warm-climate kitchen with white, blues and greens.

Warm peach walls *glow under the recessed lighting. Oak cabinets take on a light wash of color from the warm walls. Soft green, a color complementary to peach, is a subtle accent.*

Pastels. *Powdery blue-green furnishings set among neutral counters, walls and cabinets create a serene mood. The white ceiling and the wallcovering reflect light, adding a sunny, fresh feel to the room.*

Bold and beautiful. *The colors in this painted stool coordinate with the printed fabric of the placemat and the small pictures on the wall, to bring a splash of color to this bright white kitchen.*

15

For dramatic visual impact, use splashes of bold color to accent a space. Intense hues, used judiciously, will enhance the contrast in a color scheme.

Lively accent colors are an effective way to prevent neutral color schemes from becoming too subdued. Areas of strong color can also be used to emphasize eye-catching details in a room that lacks architectural interest.

Photo courtesy of Armstrong World Industries, Inc.

Bright yellow *laminate counters accent this kitchen and dining area. Black and white in solids and patterns are an effective mix. Yellow dishes set on white tables create a vibrant contrast.*

Photo courtesy of Cy DeCosse Inc.

Deep, midnight blue *countertops and walls are accented by brightly colored curtains in this traditional kitchen. The rich blue color creates a comfortable contrast to the warm tones in the cupboards, stools and woodwork around the room.*

French blue knobs, *tambour doors, counter edges and molding give a country look to traditional raised-panel cabinets. Patterns make strong accents, too. Note the plaid wallcovering, bordered with blue molding.*

Skylights/spotlights. *Two generous skylights allow the sun to flood the U-shaped kitchen. Spotlights on a track high in the vault provide general lighting. A second track brightens the cooktop area and turns a dramatic shine on counter and cabinets.*

LIGHTING

Bright looks that really cook

Curved greenhouse windows *span the work stations in an efficient galley kitchen. Cans mounted on a track (not visible) provide general lighting.*

An effective lighting plan combines general lighting with track lights and recessed ceiling fixtures. Task lighting, such as an under-cabinet fixture, is also important in kitchens for those times when you are working at the sink, cooktop or on the countertop.

Natural lighting is an important part of any kitchen plan as well. Skylights and openings high in the wall, such as clerestory or greenhouse windows, are superior sources of natural light.

Decorative accent lighting is taking a more prominent place in kitchen design. A popular choice: lighted glass-front cabinets.

Multilevel lighting is a must for efficiency in any kitchen. An overhead ceiling light, which provides general lighting, is combined with decorative task lighting over the island and recessed lights over the remaining countertops, to provide a full range of lighting options. The French patio doors also bring natural light into the kitchen during the daytime.

A glass block wall makes a dramatic difference during the daytime in this contemporary kitchen. Natural light streams in to brighten the room and provide general illumination, while a pendant light above the table and a wall sconce provide additional lighting, when needed.

Photo courtesy of Kitchens by ___

Eyeball fixtures, spaced to shine on the sink, cooktop and the walkway to the refrigerator, provide even lighting. Dramatic accent: glass blocks, lighted from inside the counter, shimmer with swirling patterns of icy light.

Photo courtesy of Crystal Cabinet Works, Inc.

An adjustable lamp can be set at the proper height for those who prefer to be seated as they work. Pull the cord, and the lamp rises for those who like to stand while working.

LIGHTING

As you plan your lighting, try to bring in as much natural light as you can. If possible, try to plan windows on at least two different walls, or use another light source, such as a skylight, patio door or even a glass block wall, to balance the illumination from a single window.

Artificial light should provide both general illumination and task lighting. There are several approaches you can take to accomplish this. One way is to use recessed lights over all the counters and work areas. They focus light where it is needed and also throw off enough ambient light to provide general illumination.

Another approach is to use an overhead fixture, such as a pendant light, for general illumination. Then arrange task lighting where needed.

Accent lighting can be used to produce special effects. Spotlight or cabinet lighting can create stunning effects and dramatic moods.

MATERIALS

The building blocks of personal style

Simplify the process of selecting materials for your kitchen by shopping for one or two basics at a time. Tackle counters or cabinets first. Flooring and wallcovering may come next.

Cabinet shopping, for example, boils down to two basic choices: wood or laminate. Research cabinet styles, then select your material. Next, define the details, such as door style, finish or color, trim and storage components.

Flooring, wallcovering and counters offer a diverse range of choices. Some of the more contemporary materials include glass block, vinyl, marble, granite or hand-painted tile.

Photo courtesy of The Amtico Company Limited

*A **custom-designed inlaid vinyl floor** achieves the elegant look of marble at the price of vinyl. Vinyl floors require minimal upkeep to stay looking great for a long time. And cooks will appreciate the softer surface vinyl provides underfoot for added comfort.*

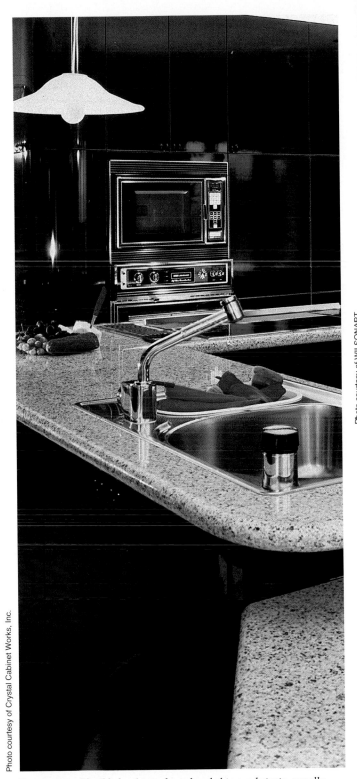

Photo courtesy of Crystal Cabinet Works, Inc.

Photo courtesy of WILSONART

Solid-surface material. *Man-made sheets, up to ¾ inch thick, rival the good looks of granite and marble. Sheets may be cut and shaped like wood. It is an expensive product, but it is durable and resists stains and burns.*

Photo courtesy of WILSONART

Laminates. *Flexible laminate sheets bonded to a substrate, usually particle board, make durable counters and cabinets. An array of dazzling colors and patterns is on the market. Above, dramatic high-gloss black laminate is bonded to curved cabinets.*

(right) **Ceramic tile surfaces** *create an eye-catching kitchen that's both functionally and aesthetically appealing. The natural color of the tile is an excellent complement to the olive green cabinets.*

Photo courtesy of Armstrong World Industries, Inc.

Glass block, *once a utilitarian material for basement and bathroom windows, now has a place in high-tech interiors. Glass block transmits light, creates stunning visual patterns and is suitable for structural uses such as the counter base shown above.*

Photo courtesy of Elkay Manufacturing Co.

Solid-surface sinks *are made in a variety of styles and shapes to make their long-lasting beauty available for any kitchen.*

Photo courtesy of WILSONART

Granite-textured laminate *is cut into strips and applied to a curved sliding door. Custom cabinets like this add eye-catching detail.*

Photo courtesy of WILSONART

Perma-Edge® edging *lets you dress up ordinary laminate and mask resin lines.*

Ceramic tile. Customize counters at a moderate cost with patterned tile, tile borders or designs created from tiles of different sizes and colors. Grout colored to match the tile is easier to clean than white grout. Above, earthy tile with floral insets creates a warm kitchen.

Marble tile in high-gloss black with a fine, white grain makes the island the centerpiece of this two-tone kitchen. Marble is a material that complements both traditional and contemporary decors.

STORAGE IDEAS

Space-saving storage ideas

Storage systems in wood, metal or plastic are optional accessories in most cabinet lines. Select storage components that fit your budget and cooking style.

The following storage principles will help you organize your kitchen more efficiently.

Store items at the point of use. For example, locate pots and pans in drawers or on heavy-duty pull-out shelves near the cooktop. Fit storage to the items stored, such as divided cutlery trays for silverware.

If you want decorative appeal, try a colorful kitchenware display or hang shiny copper pots and pans overhead. Open storage visually enlarges a room, making it a wise choice for smaller kitchens.

Use every cubic inch of storage space. Don't waste space between shelves. A few of the excellent storage ideas available today are illustrated in the photos below and right.

Pull-out trays *store cleaning supplies, brushes and nonrefrigerated vegetables in sink base. Tilt-down sink panel turns wasted space into a storage area for pads, sponges and other supplies used at the sink.*

Linen trays. *Shallow sliding trays store linens without wrinkling the fabric. Ideal for tablecloths, placemats and cloth napkins.*

Swing-up shelf *is an ideal way to store less frequently used appliances, like this large mixer.*

Spice pantry and drawer. *Island storage puts spices and cooking ingredients within reach of the cooktop. Spice pantry is a fine example of sizing storage to the containers stored. The pull-out drawer allows full use of a deep cabinet.*

Roll-out serving cart *glides out from under counter. The three-tier cart is hidden by a false cabinet door when stored. A space-saving accessory for entertaining.*

Photo courtesy of Wood-Mode Cabinetry

Roll-out table *is a big asset for small kitchens. It doubles as a counter or a table for two. Its lower work surface is ideal for pastry preparation. For storage, the hinged false drawer in the counter is lifted and the tabletop slides in; the table legs fit in recesses flanking the base cabinet.*

Photo courtesy of Wood-Mode Cabinetry

Photo courtesy of Crystal Cabinet Works, Inc.

Bread drawer, *a fixture in kitchens in the days before preservatives, is lined with metal and ventilated to keep bread fresh. Pair a bread drawer with a cutting board to create a handy sandwich bar.*

Corner cabinet trays *rotate, bringing a collection of crockery into view. The wedge-shaped trays fit exactly on the shelves.*

Round cabinet/sliding doors. Behind tambour style doors are curved shelves for pots and pans, which are stored directly below the cooktop.

Round cabinet/hinged doors. Ultracontemporary island features curved laminate doors with European-style concealed hinges.

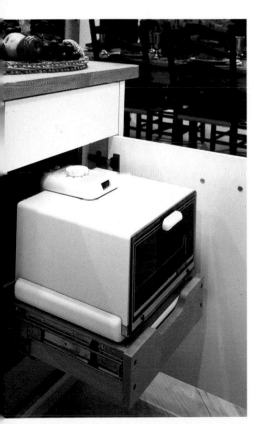

Pull-out appliance drawer frees valuable counter space. Full-extension slides ensure proper support for heavier appliances.

Appliance garage. Handsome trio of appliance garages with brass tambour doors saves on counter workspace. Two storage nooks hold coffee-making equipment, while a pull-out swivel shelf houses a portable TV.

29

Multilevel storage. *Pantry with adjustable metal storage baskets is a cook's dream. Every can and package is visible. The tall storage racks in the lower section of the pantry rotate so the shelving behind is easily accessible.*

Pull-out pantry *fits neatly into a corner, flush with the laminate desk. Plastic-coated metal storage baskets hung on hooks provide flexible storage.*

Island pantry is a wood variation of the multilevel storage system. Two door racks and the rotating racks inside have space-expanding adjustable shelves. A bonus: narrow shelves at the back of the cabinet are adjustable too.

Pull-out table topped with a cutting board is part of a complete baking center. In the upper cabinet are baking supplies, utensil racks, and a mixer plugged in and ready to use. Below the table, attractive wood drawers hold bake ware.

Wood pantry, which is more expensive than most basket storage systems, is a top choice for kitchens with fine wood cabinets. This pantry features a semicircular lazy susan in the upper cabinet, with adjustable shelves and rotating racks below.

APPLIANCES & FIXTURES

Today's appliances offer features to fit every lifestyle. Cooktops with inserts for grills, griddles, deep fryers and rotisseries are available; refrigerator/freezers come in dozens of sizes and configurations; stainless steel, solid-surface and ceramic sinks now have one, two or three basins, along with numerous styles of faucets, sprayers and other attachments. And you can find ceramic and solid-surface materials in the latest colors. Down-sized appliances for small kitchens also are available.

A cleanup center is a top priority of almost every busy kitchen. Because up to 50% of your time in the kitchen is spent here, it's smart to pay special attention to sinks, faucets, and related items.

Cooktops add flexibility for special needs. Standard units come in gas or electric, and in finishes that include stainless steel, enameled cast iron or glass. Often you can interchange burners with a grill, a griddle or other specialty items.

Custom accessories turn an ordinary kitchen sink into a convenient work center. Cutting board insert, colander and mini drain board are just some of the options available.

Gourmet island. A budding gourmet can take cooking lessons at this TV/VCR center. With the swiveling TV, the cook can follow recipe directions, in sequence, as he or she moves to work stations around the island. Details: black octagon sink, built-in wine rack, cookbook shelves, multiple storage drawers.

Wine cooler is a component of a beverage serving center. Other mini-refrigerators are designed for installation in island and base cabinets.

Corner sink *expands design possibilities for the small kitchen. The deep, single-bowl sink is located where it is most useful: between the dishwasher and the food preparation counter. An ideal fixture for a one-cook kitchen.*

Microwave/vent hood. *Multipurpose microwave has cooktop task lights and vents in its base. A low-profile vent hood for contemporary kitchens.*

(right) **Built-in refrigerator** *fits neatly into a custom cabinet with overhead storage. Bonus: wooden panels on refrigerator door match the rustic cabinetry.*

Commercial-style range *has four high-temperature gas burners, a griddle and a large oven. Textured range hood hides lights and powerful exhaust fans.*

KITCHEN
IDEAS

The fresh, contemporary colors and the country flavor are a winning combination in this contemporary country kitchen. The soothing colors provide the perfect background for the sleek Euro-style cabinets. Accents like shiny copper pots and pans and decorative bottles add a subtle country influence.

Photo courtesy of Bruce Hardwood Floors

TRADITIONAL
Classically comfortable designs

A traditional room is inspired by the past and its time-honored decorations. From elegant and formal to simple and whimsical, the common thread throughout traditional design is comfort.

The cabinetwork sets the tone of a traditional kitchen. It is a showplace for finely crafted wood cabinetry. With many styles to choose from, the design may be simple and plain or detailed with elaborate moldings and panels. The type of wood used also influences the look of the finished cabinet. Oak, walnut and cherry are popular because of their distinctive grain.

Features like deep crown molding, roomy pantries, open shelving, appliances customized with wood front panels and glass cabinets are hallmarks of traditional styling. Accent with gleaming brass and copper accessories. You can also make a dramatic statement with colors and textures. Fabrics most often found in traditional kitchens are polished cottons patterned in florals, paisleys or stripes.

TRADITIONAL

Today we appreciate the furniture and accessories of the past for features like solid design and attention to detail. A traditional kitchen has a sense of sentimentality that is expressed through collectibles like classical figures, bottled ships or family heirlooms. A traditional Victorian look can be achieved with the materials used in window treatments and wallpapers. Flowing draperies, shirred valances, shutters and swags are ways to create a traditional window dressing.

The way you accessorize a traditional kitchen adds to its overall richness. Bring life to a kitchen with lush ivy or flowers. Fill a traditional iron pot rack with polished copper pans, and hang a ceiling fixture of brass and glass.

Another necessary ingredient for classic kitchen design is practical storage space. In a traditional kitchen, this might include glass-fronted cupboards, which can also be used as attractive displays.

Traditional design details are featured in the wood paneling and decorative moldings of the cupboards and center island. Brass handles on the cupboards and brass fixtures on the sinks bring out the beauty of the polished copper pans hanging from the traditional iron pot rack, and enhance the classic charm of this kitchen.

Photo courtesy of Kraftmaid Inc.

Select wood cabinetry for a warm contemporary look. Sleek European cabinets are available in a variety of hardwoods and stained finishes. Consider other uses of wood: on butcher-block counters, for cabinet trim and pulls, on light fixtures, around windows and doors.

Photo courtesy of Bruce Hardwood Floors

The cool, classic look of marble is incorporated into the countertops, providing a decorative yet durable surface for the island and countertops of this kitchen. The elegant look of marble is continued in the faux marble design of the vinyl floor. Plenty of counter space for food preparation and ample seating are provided.

Traditional with a twist. *The interesting and unusual shape of this center island follows the floor plan of this colorful kitchen; its generous size provides a place for storing pots and pans on one side and open shelves on another.*

TRADITIONAL

Islands that fit your lifestyle

Kitchens of the last century were dominated by a large, central work table. Today, the kitchen island replaces that old-fashioned table. An island expands counter space, increases storage capacity and provides an area for casual dining.

Drop in a cooktop with down-draft ventilation, plumb a second sink or wire an electric outlet in the island. For entertaining, invite guests to sit at the island while dinner is being prepared.

COUNTRY
Charming Country Kitchens

Country means comfort, great food, good company. The country kitchen is a relaxed, informal room that combines modern convenience with easygoing charm. Define the style with naturals like pine cabinets, plank flooring, willow baskets and stoneware.

Fill your country haven with heirloom quilts and hand-carved furnishings or displays of collectibles. Country mixes well with almost any style, from Victorian to contemporary, so it's easy to modify the look of your country kitchen.

Photo courtesy of Armstrong World Industries, Inc.

Hefty beams and posts *set a country mood. Weathered cabinets with wrought-iron hinges conceal the refrigerator and provide storage. An antique woodstove shares kitchen duty with a modern cooktop. Overhead, a lively collection of baskets and cookware.*

Rustic furniture *incorporates authentic tree limbs for an eye-catching addition to this clever country kitchen. The weathered look of the color-washed cabinetry seems right at home next to a modern sink and faucet. Live plants, decorative baskets and copper cooking utensils add to the collective country look of this kitchen.*

Updated country kitchen combines tile counters and rich oak cabinets with massive beams and vintage kitchenalia. Flavor the mix of old and new with whitewashed walls and a cooktop set into a curved alcove.

The friendly feel of a country kitchen is warm and comfortable. Filled with handcrafted furniture, natural textures and charming collectibles, country kitchens offer a sense of hospitality.

Country can also span many moods and varying styles. Spacious farmhouse kitchens have solid construction, stone, brick or tile floors and often a network of smaller storage rooms or pantries. The functional French country kitchen centers around food and its preparation, with shelves filled with spices and seasonings, and cooking utensils scattered about. American country brings to mind the image of large, rough ceiling beams, hand stenciling, stucco, glazed crockery, copper pots, linen and gingham and baking bread.

Hearty country cooking requires pots and pans in abundance. A handsome display of gleaming cookware hangs from butcher hooks on a sturdy pot rack above the island. Plate rack shows off Colonial-era pewter dishes.

Smooth laminate cabinets and shiny chrome furniture set the contemporary tone in this kitchen. The laminate cabinets are a soft, two-tone beige that is repeated in the refrigerator as well. The faux marble design of the vinyl floor adds to the appeal of this sophisticated setting.

CONTEMPORARY

Sleek and streamlined, a contemporary kitchen follows the design adage, "form follows function." Soothing curves, understated background colors and exciting textures combine to create a mood that's sophisticated, yet soft; worldly, yet warm.

A new chapter in kitchen design began when traditional cabinets were manufactured with light or natural finishes. Cabinet construction has been updated, too. Many styles are frameless, so doors and drawers fit flush; no cabinet frame is visible. The cabinetry blends beautifully with contemporary patterns and colors in wallcovering, flooring and window treatments.

Photo courtesy of Mannington Mills, Inc.

Photo courtesy of Crystal Cabinet Works, Inc.

The most efficient floor plan: *an L-shaped kitchen with island. The refrigerator, sink and cooktop are within easy reach. The solid-surface counters and white ceramic tile island lighten the room. Wood panels camouflage the refrigerator and dishwasher.*

Contemporary kitchens are free of clutter. Countertops and cabinets are bare and streamlined. Cabinets in modern kitchens are usually frameless, and often covered with laminate. Countertops generally consist of a solid-surface material, a slab stone like marble, or stainless steel—or they are finished with laminate.

Kitchens with a contemporary design are laid out to make limited space more efficient and usable. Windows have minimal treatments or are left untrimmed, and kitchen equipment is hidden out of sight to help maintain the uncluttered look.

The ultracontemporary design of the inlaid vinyl floor brings the look of the future to this Euro-style kitchen.

Photo courtesy of The Amtico Company Limited

Contemporary neoclassic style sets the mood in this monotone kitchen. Black marble countertops and black lacquer in the dining room furniture and barstools add a formal accent to the natural wood cabinetry.

White: pure and simple provides a fresh, crisp look that is carried throughout the room. The materials that create the contemporary style are often in the form of ceramic tiles, laminate countertops and vinyl floor coverings.

In modern kitchens, the emphasis is on function. They are efficient and easy to maintain. Because many of the appliances are built in and compact, a contemporary design is a wise choice for a small kitchen.

(below) **Silverware holders** beautifully accessorize any table. Depending on the materials used, they can have a simple tailored look or, with lace trim added, a more Victorian look, as shown here.

Focal point. *Gleaming copper and brass hood is the centerpiece of this kitchen, set off by white raised-panel cabinets, white counter and floor. Brass rails and cabinet pulls shine under recessed lights.*

CONTEMPORARY

Regional style. *Southwestern galley kitchen tucked behind adobe fireplace mixes sleek European cabinets with rustic counters. Regional elements: rough ceiling beams, carved stool and plank shelving lined with copper cookware, baskets and earthy pottery.*

(photo left) **Smooth lines** *of the European-style cabinetry give this kitchen a contemporary quality. Traditional accents like a pewter teapot on the stovetop are sprinkled throughout.*

Kitchen Remodeling Basics

Create new floor plans to help you visualize kitchen improvements. There also are computer software programs available that make this easy to do. Experiment with different arrangements, and indicate all countertop measurements on each plan. Note how different arrangements affect the classic kitchen "work triangle."

Principles of Kitchen Design

As you begin to plan your new kitchen, keep in mind the principles of kitchen design. Use these principles to help identify problem areas in your present kitchen, and to help evaluate the efficiency of your new kitchen.

Establish work areas. A kitchen has three major work areas for: 1) food preparation, including the refrigerator and food storage cabinets; 2) cooking, built around the range/oven and the microwave; and 3) cleanup, combining the sink, dishwasher, and garbage disposer.

The kitchen work triangle. A triangular arrangement of work areas is the classic of kitchen design. It helps make efficient use of food preparation, cooking, and cleanup areas. To create the kitchen triangle, add together the distances between the major work areas. The total should be no less than 12 feet and no more than 21 feet. A smaller triangle means the work spaces are too crowded. A larger triangle indicates that steps are wasted.

Plan adequate counter space. For example, there should be an area next to the refrigerator to place and unload grocery bags. Also, there should be space next to cooking appliances for food preparation, and a place next to the sink for stacking dishes. The recommended minimums are: 24

Experiment with Different Designs

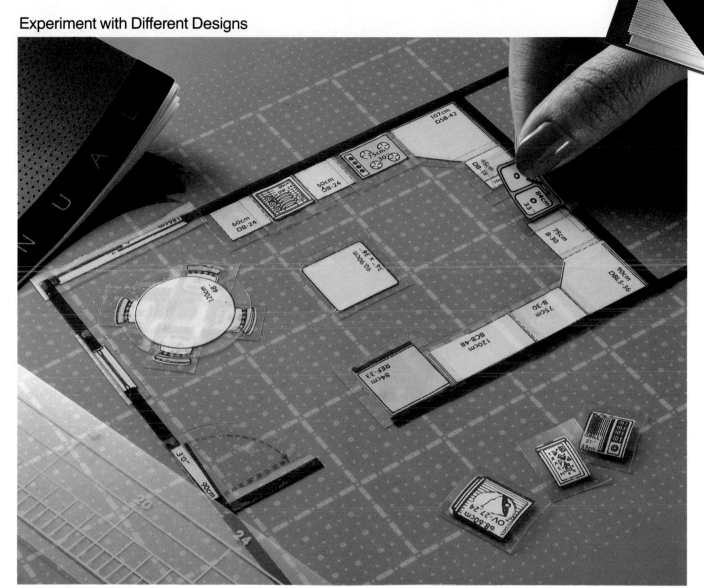

Use a planning system, like this modular, reusable design kit, to help you visualize the placement of new cabinets or appliances. Use your floor plan to establish the shape of your kitchen and to help plan the solutions to any problem areas.

inches on each side of cooking appliances; 24 inches on each side of the sink area; 18 inches next to a refrigerator.

Store items for easy access. Cabinets near any one work area should contain related items. Place small appliances such as a blender or toaster in the food preparation area. Store seldom-used items separately. If your cabinet space is inadequate, consider adding low-cost cabinet organizers, like roll-out shelves and baskets, or door racks for canned goods. If you decide to install new major appliances, make sure you plan storage space near the appliance site.

If your project calls for rearranging the placement of your cabinets, experiment with new floor plans.

A kitchen design kit, available at bookstores and home improvement centers, helps create new designs. You may want to discuss your final plans with a Certified Kitchen Designer (CKD) or an architect. For a fee, a professional can evaluate the design, draw detail specifications, and prepare a complete materials list.

Establish a work schedule. The time it takes to alter a kitchen, no matter how brief, is a disruption of the home and family routine. Plan ways to store food, cook meals, and wash dishes while work is being completed. If you hire professionals for portions of the job, be sure to get estimates for time as well as materials and labor. Obtain all necessary building permits for the portions of the work you will do yourself.

Straightedge

Sanding block

Putty knives

Utility knife

Handscrew

Standard screwdriver

Phillips screwdriver

Dust mask

Safety glasses

Nail set

16-oz. claw hammer

Wonderbar®

Crosscut saw

Framing square

Combination square

C-clamps

SANDVIK

Bar clamp

Pencil

Tape measure

Chalk line

Caulk gun

2' carpenter's level

Tools

A collection of quality tools does not require a large initial investment. A homeowner can build a tool collection by buying tools as they are needed for each project. Invest in top-grade tools made by reputable manufacturers. A quality tool always carries a full warranty.

Basic hand tools (photo, page opposite) are essential for the completion of most of the kitchen remodeling described in this book. A quality hand tool can last a lifetime, and over the years will be used many times for repairs and home improvement projects.

Basic power tools (photo, below) can increase the speed and precision of your kitchen improvement projects. Many power tools are made in cordless versions. Cordless tools can be used anywhere and are not restricted by electrical power connections.

When purchasing power tools, read specification labels to compare features. More horsepower, faster motor speeds, and higher amperage ratings indicate a well-engineered tool. Better-quality tools also have roller or ball bearings instead of sleeve bearings.

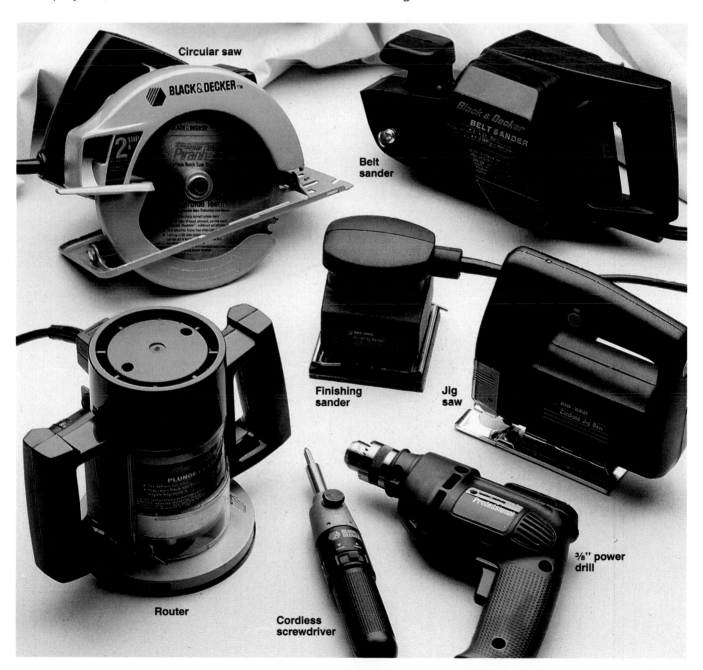

Circular saw

Belt sander

Finishing sander

Jig saw

Router

Cordless screwdriver

3/8" power drill

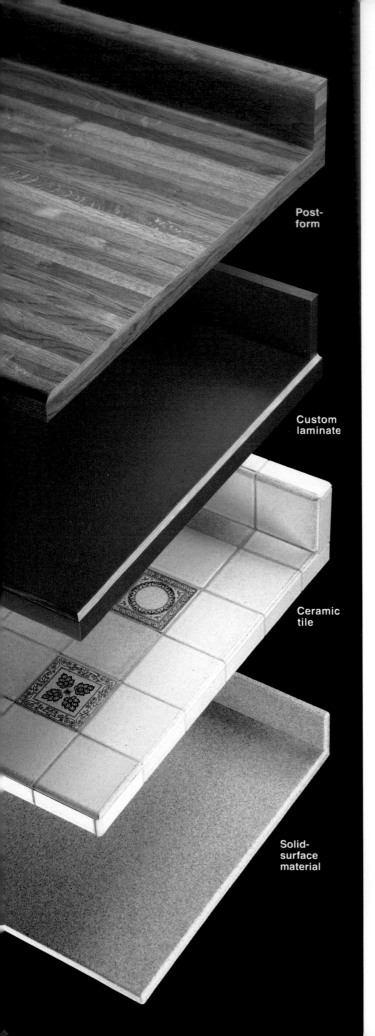

Post-form

Custom laminate

Ceramic tile

Solid-surface material

Countertops

Countertops provide the main workspace in a kitchen, so they must be made from durable and easy-to-clean materials. Countertops add color, pattern, texture, and shape to kitchens, so choose a style that harmonizes with the other elements in the room.

Post-form countertops are made of sheet laminates glued to particleboard, and come from the factory ready to install. Post-form countertops have pre-attached backsplashes and front edge treatments. They are manufactured in a variety of colors and styles.

Custom laminate countertops are built by gluing sheet laminates to particleboard. Laminates are available in hundreds of colors and patterns to match any kitchen decorating scheme. Special edge treatments can be added to customize a laminate countertop.

Ceramic tile is especially durable and creates a beautiful surface that resists spills and stains. Tile is available in a wide range of styles and prices, and creating a ceramic tile countertop is an excellent do-it-yourself project.

Solid-surface materials are manufactured from acrylic or polyester resins mixed with additives and formed into sheets that are ¼", ½", or ¾" thick. Solid-surface materials are expensive, but they are tough and easy to maintain. They can be cut and shaped with woodworking tools.

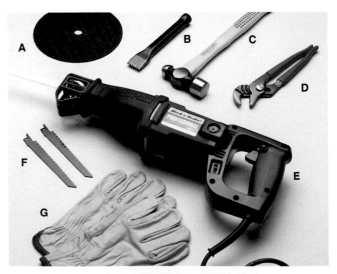

Specialty tools & supplies for removing countertops include: masonry-cutting circular saw blade (A), masonry chisel (B), ball peen hammer (C), channel-type pliers (D), reciprocating saw (E) with coarse wood-cutting blade (F), work gloves (G).

How to Remove an Old Countertop

1 Turn off water at shutoff valves. Disconnect and remove plumbing fixtures and appliances. Remove any brackets or screws holding the countertop to the cabinets. Unscrew the take-up bolts on mitered countertops (page 69).

2 Use a utility knife to cut caulk beads along backsplash and edge of countertop. Remove any trim. Using a flat pry bar, try to lift countertop away from base cabinets.

3 If countertop cannot be pried up, use a reciprocating saw or jig saw with coarse wood-cutting blade to cut the countertop into pieces for removal. Be careful not to cut into base cabinets.

Ceramic tile: Wear eye protection. Chisel tile away from the base with a masonry chisel and ball peen hammer. A tile countertop that has a mortar bed can be cut into pieces with a circular saw and abrasive masonry-cutting blade.

Installing a
Post-form Countertop

Post-form laminate countertops come in stock
lengths, and are cut to fit your kitchen space. Pre-
mitered sections are available for two- or three-piece
countertops that continue around corners. If the
countertop has an exposed end, you will need
an endcap kit that contains a preshaped strip of
matching laminate.

For a precise fit, the backsplash must be trimmed
to fit any unevenness in the back wall. This process is called scribing. Post-form countertops
have a narrow strip of laminate on the backsplash
for scribing.

Everything You Need:

Basic Hand Tools (page 62): tape measure, framing square, pencil, straightedge, C-clamps,
hammer, level, caulk gun.

Basic Power Tools (page 63): jig saw, belt sander,
drill and spade bit, cordless screwdriver.

Basic Materials: post-form countertop sections.

Specialty Tools & Materials: photo, page opposite.

How to Install a Post-form Countertop

1 Measure span of base cabinets, from corner to
outside edge of cabinet. Add 1″ for overhang if
end will be exposed. If an end will butt against an
appliance, subtract 1/16″ to prevent scratches.

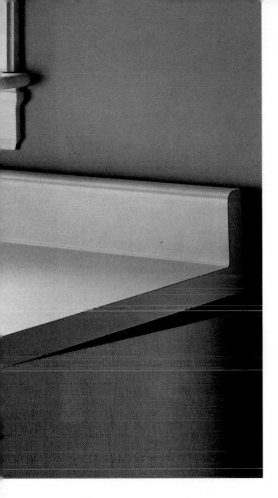

Specialty tools & supplies include: wood shims (A), take-up bolts (B), wallboard screws (C), wire brads (D), household iron (E), endcap laminate (Γ), endcap battens (G), silicone caulk (H), file (I), adjustable wrench (J), carpenter's glue (K), buildup blocks (L), scribing compass (M).

2 Use a framing square to mark a cutting line on the bottom surface of the countertop. Cut off the countertop with a jig saw, using a clamped straight-edge as a guide.

3 Attach battens from endcap kit to edge of counter-top, using carpenter's glue and small brads. Sand out any unevenness with belt sander.

(continued next page)

4 Hold endcap laminate against end, slightly over-lapping edges. Activate adhesive by pressing an iron set at medium heat against endcap. Cool with wet cloth, then file endcap laminate flush with edges.

5 Position countertop on base cabinets. Make sure front edge of countertop is parallel to cabinet face. Check countertop for level. Make sure that drawers and doors open and close freely. If needed, adjust countertop with wood shims.

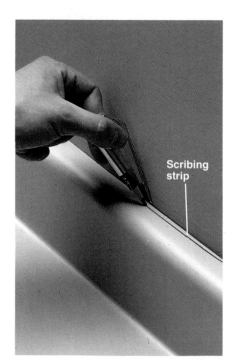

6 Because walls are usually un-even, use a compass to trace wall outline onto backsplash scribing strip. Set compass arms to match widest gap, then move compass along length of the wall to transfer outline to scribing strip.

7 Remove countertop. Use belt sander to grind backsplash to scribe line.

8 Mark cutout for self-rimming sink. Position sink upside down on countertop and trace outline. Remove sink and draw cutting line ⅝" inside sink outline. To install sink, see page 144.

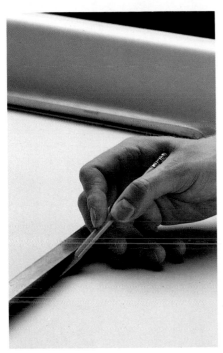 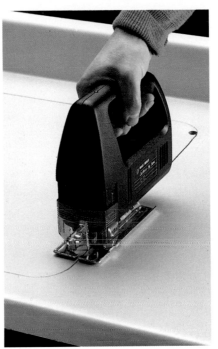 

9 Mark cutout for cooktop or sink with frame. Position metal frame on countertop, and trace outline around edge of vertical flange. Remove frame. To install a framed cooktop or sink, see page 144.

10 Drill pilot hole just inside cutting line. Make cutouts with jig saw. Support cutout area from below so that falling cutout does not damage cabinet.

11 Apply a bead of silicone caulk on edges of mitered countertop sections. Force countertop pieces tightly together.

 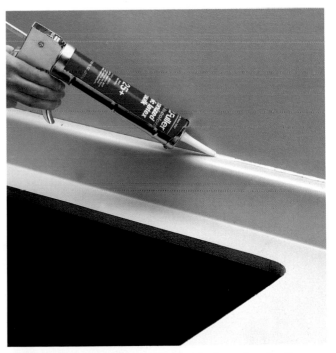

12 From underneath cabinet, install and tighten miter take-up bolts. Position countertop tightly against wall and fasten to cabinets by driving wallboard screws up through corner brackets into the countertop (page 83). Screws should be long enough to provide maximum holding power, but not long enough to puncture laminate surface.

13 Seal seam between backsplash and wall with acrylic caulk. Smooth bead with a wet fingertip. Wipe away excess caulk.

Building a Custom Laminate Countertop

Build your own durable, beautiful countertop with plastic sheet laminates. Plastic laminates are available in hundreds of colors, styles, and textures. A countertop made with laminates can be tailored to fit any space, and can be customized with a decorative edge treatment (page 78).

Laminates are sold in 6-, 8-, 10-, or 12-foot lengths that are about $\frac{1}{20}$" thick. Laminate sheets range in width from 30" to 48". Most laminates are made by bonding a thin surface layer of colored resins. Another type of laminate has consistent color through the thickness of the sheet. Solid-color laminate countertops do not show dark lines at the trimmed edges, but they chip more easily than traditional laminates and must be handled carefully.

Choose nonflammable contact cement when building a countertop, and thoroughly ventilate your work area.

Everything You Need:

Basic Hand Tools (page 62): tape measure, framing square, pencil, straightedge, clamps, caulk gun.

Basic Power Tools (page 63): circular saw with combination blade, cordless screwdriver, belt sander, router.

Basic Materials: ¾" particleboard, sheet laminate.

Specialty Tools & Materials: photo, page opposite.

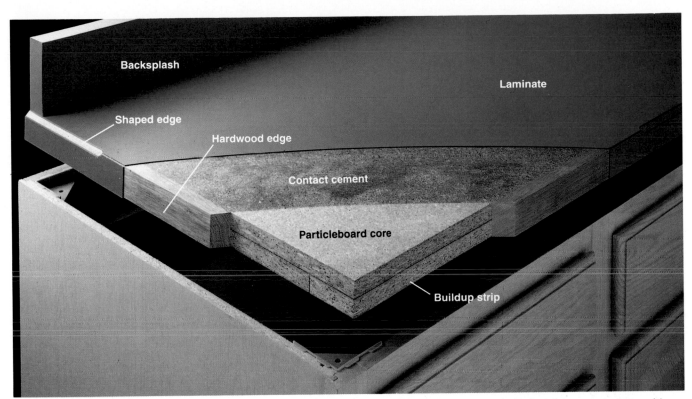

Laminate countertop: Countertop core is ¾" particleboard. Perimeter is built up with strips of particleboard screwed to the bottom of the core. For decorative edge treatments, hardwood strips can be attached to core.

Laminate pieces are bonded to the countertop with contact cement. Edges are trimmed and shaped with a router.

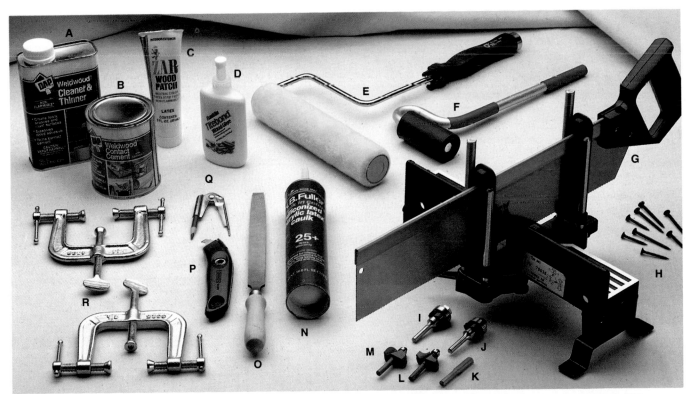

Specialty tools & supplies include: contact cement thinner (A), contact cement (B), latex wood patch (C), carpenter's glue (D), paint roller (E), J-roller (F), miter box (G), wallboard screws (H), flush-cutting router bit (I), 15° bevel-cutting router bit (J), straight router bit (K), corner rounding router bit (L), cove router bit (M), silicone caulk (N), file (O), scoring tool (P), scribing compass (Q), 3-way clamps (R).

How to Build a Custom Laminate Countertop

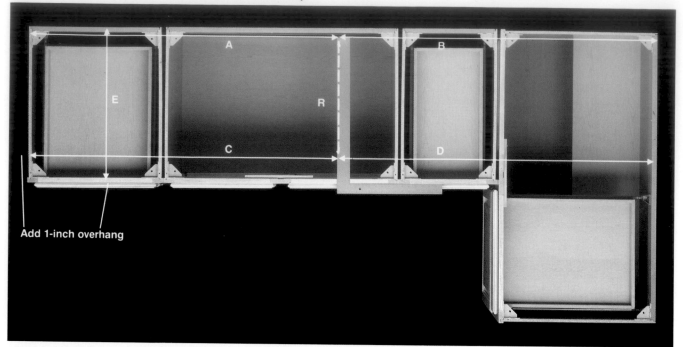

Add 1-inch overhang

1 Measure along tops of base cabinets to determine size of countertop. If wall corners are not square, use a framing square to establish a reference line (R) near middle of base cabinets, perpendicular to front of cabinets. Take four measurements (A, B, C, D) from reference line to cabinet ends. Allow for overhangs by adding 1" to the length for each exposed end, and 1" to the width (E). If an end butts against an appliance, subtract 1/16" from length to prevent scratching appliance.

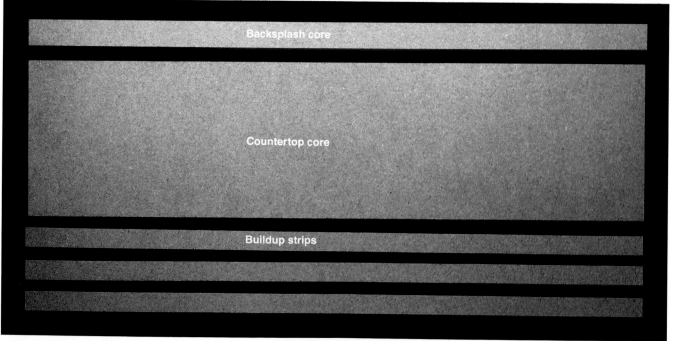

Backsplash core

Countertop core

Buildup strips

2 Transfer measurements from step 1, using a framing square to establish a reference line. Cut core to size using a circular saw with clamped straightedge as a guide. Cut 4" strips of particleboard for backsplash, and for joint support where sections of countertop core are butted together. Cut 3" strips for edge buildups.

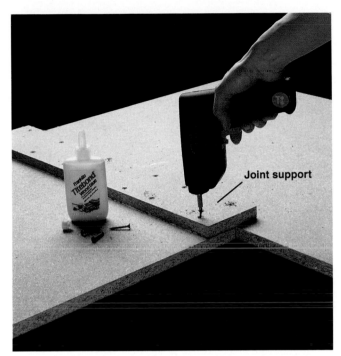

Joint support

3 Join the countertop core pieces on the bottom side. Attach a 4" particleboard joint support across the seam, using carpenter's glue and 1¼" wallboard screws.

Buildup strips

4 Attach 3" edge buildup strips to bottom of countertop, using 1¼" wallboard screws. Fill any gaps on outside edges with latex wood patch, then sand edges with belt sander. (For decorative edge treatments, see page 78.)

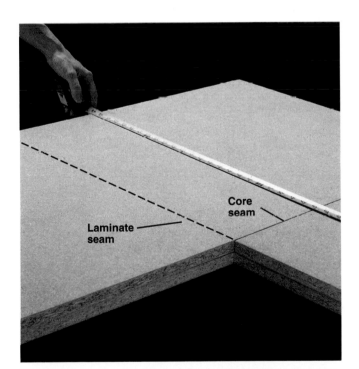

Laminate seam

Core seam

5 To determine the size of the laminate top, measure countertop core. For strength, laminate seams should run opposite to core seam. Add ½" trimming margin to both the length and width of each piece. Measure laminate needed for face and edges of backsplash, and for exposed edges of countertop core. Add ½" to each measurement.

6 Cut laminate by scoring and breaking it. Draw a cutting line, then etch along the line with a scoring tool. Use a straightedge as a guide. Two passes of scoring tool will help laminate break cleanly.

(continued next page)

7 Bend laminate toward the scored line until the sheet breaks cleanly. For better control on narrow pieces, clamp a straightedge along scored line before bending laminate. Wear gloves to avoid being cut by sharp edges.

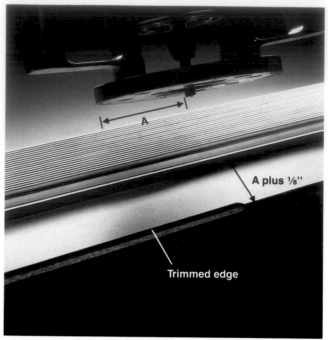

8 Create tight-fitting seams with plastic laminate by using a router and a straight bit to trim edges that will butt together. Measure from cutting edge of the bit to edge of the router baseplate (A). Place laminate on scrap wood and align edges. To guide the router, clamp a straightedge on the laminate at distance A plus ⅛", parallel to laminate edge. Trim laminate.

9 Apply laminate to sides of countertop first. Using a paint roller, apply two coats of contact cement to edge of countertop and one coat to back of laminate. Let cement dry according to manufacturer's directions. Position laminate carefully, then press against edge of countertop. Bond with J-roller.

10 Use a router and flush-cutting bit to trim edge strip flush with top and bottom surfaces of countertop core. At edges where router cannot reach, trim excess laminate with a file. Apply laminate to remaining edges, and trim with router.

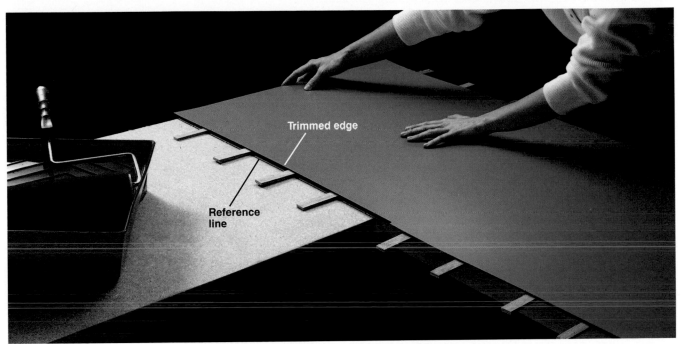

Trimmed edge

Reference line

11 Test-fit laminate top on countertop core. Check that laminate overhangs all edges. At seam locations, draw a reference line on core where laminate edges will butt together. Remove laminate. Make sure all surfaces are free of dust, then apply one coat of contact cement to back of laminate and two coats to core. Place spacers made of ¼''-thick scrap wood at 6'' intervals across countertop core. Because contact cement bonds instantly, spacers allow laminate to be positioned accurately over core without bonding. Align laminate with seam reference line. Beginning at one end, remove spacers and press laminate to countertop core.

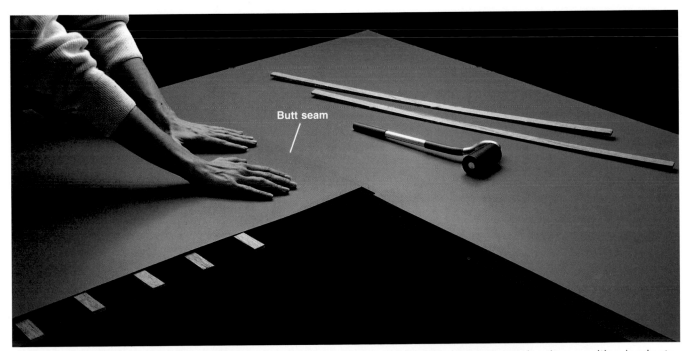

Butt seam

12 Apply contact cement to remaining core and next piece of laminate. Let cement dry, then position laminate on spacers, and carefully align butt seam. Beginning at seam edge, remove spacers and press laminate to countertop core.

(continued next page)

13 Roll entire surface with J-roller to bond laminate to core. Clean off any excess contact cement with a soft cloth and contact cement thinner.

14 Remove excess laminate with a router and flush-cutting bit. At edges where router cannot reach, trim excess laminate with a file. Countertop is now ready for final trimming with bevel-cutting bit.

15 Finish-trim the edges with a router and 15° bevel-cutting bit. Set bit depth so that bevel edge is cut only on top laminate layer. Bit should not cut into vertical edge surface.

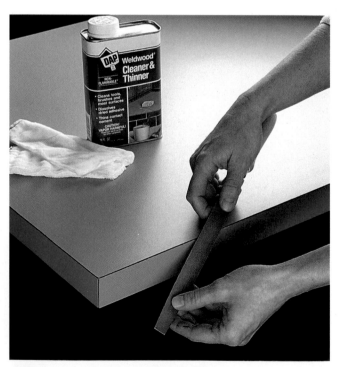

16 File all edges smooth. Use downward file strokes to avoid chipping the laminate.

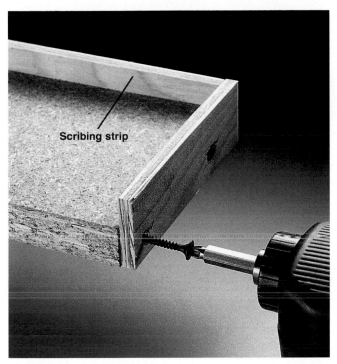

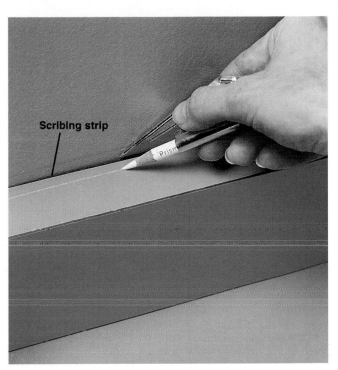

17 Cut 1¼''-wide strips of ¼'' plywood to form overhanging scribing strip for backsplash. Attach to top and sides of backsplash core with glue and wallboard screws. Cut laminate pieces and apply to exposed sides, top, and front of backsplash. Trim each piece as it is applied.

18 Test-fit countertop and backsplash. Because walls may be uneven, use compass to trace wall outline onto backsplash scribing strip. Use a belt sander to grind backsplash to scribe line (page 68).

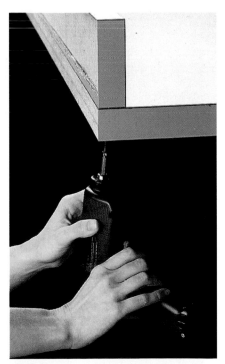

19 Apply a bead of silicone caulk to the bottom edge of the backsplash.

20 Position the backsplash on the countertop, and clamp it into place with bar clamps. Wipe away excess caulk, and let dry completely.

21 Screw 2'' wallboard screws through countertop into backsplash core. Make sure screwheads are countersunk completely for a tight fit against the base cabinet.

Solid hardwood edge

Coved edge

Rounded edge

Custom Wood Countertop Edges

For an elegant added touch on a laminate countertop, add hardwood edges and shape them with a router. Rout the edges before attaching the backsplash to the countertop.

Everything You Need:

Basic Hand Tools (page 62): hammer, nail set.

Basic Power Tools (page 63): belt sander with 120-grit sanding belt, router.

Basic Materials: 1 × 2 hardwood strips.

Specialty Tools & Supplies: (photo, page 71): carpenter's glue, finish nails, 3-way clamps, router bits.

How to Build Coved Hardwood Edges

1 Cut 1 × 2 hardwood strips to fit edges of countertop. Sand strips smooth. Miter-cut inside and outside corners.

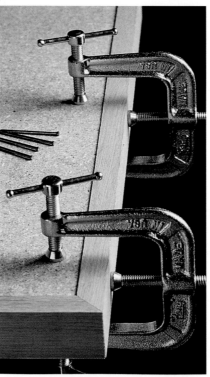

2 Attach edge strips to countertop with carpenter's glue and 3-way clamps. Drill pilot holes, then attach strip with finish nails. Recess nail heads with a nail set.

3 Sand edge strips flush with top surface of countertop, using a belt sander and 120-grit sandpaper.

How to Build Solid Hardwood Edges

1 Laminate top of countertop before attaching edge strip. Attach the edge strip flush with the surface of laminate, using carpenter's glue and finish nails (page opposite).

Corner rounding bit

2 Mold top and bottom edges of strip with router and edging bit, if desired. Stain and finish wood as desired.

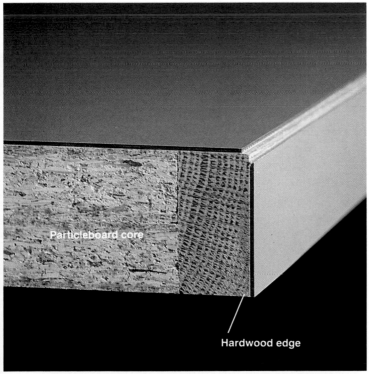

Particleboard core

Hardwood edge

4 Apply laminate to edge and top of countertop after hardwood edge has been sanded flush.

Piloted cove bit

5 Cut cove edge with a router and cove bit with ball-bearing pilot. Smooth cove with 220-grit sandpaper. Stain and finish exposed wood as desired.

Building a Ceramic Tile Countertop

Modern adhesives make it easy for a homeowner to install ceramic tile on a kitchen countertop and backsplash. Because kitchen surfaces are exposed to water, use moisture-resistant adhesive and glazed tiles. Tiles may be sold individually or in mosaic sheets attached to mesh backing. Some tiles have edge lugs that automatically set the width of grout joints. For smooth-edged tiles, use plastic spacers to maintain even grout joints.

A successful tile job requires a solid, flat base and careful planning. Dry-fit the tile job to make sure the finished layout is pleasing to the eye. After installation, seal the tile and grout with a quality silicone sealer to prevent water damage. Clean and reseal the tile periodically to maintain a new appearance.

Everything You Need:

Basic Hand Tools (page 62): tape measure, pencil, putty knife, framing square, caulk gun, hammer.

Basic Power Tools (page 63): circular saw, cordless screwdriver, orbital sander.

Basic Materials: ceramic tile, ¾" exterior (CDX) plywood, wood strips.

Specialty Tools & Materials: photo, page 82.

Ceramic tiles are available individually, or connected with mesh backing to form mosaic sheets. Ask your dealer to recommend tiles that will stand up to heavy countertop use.

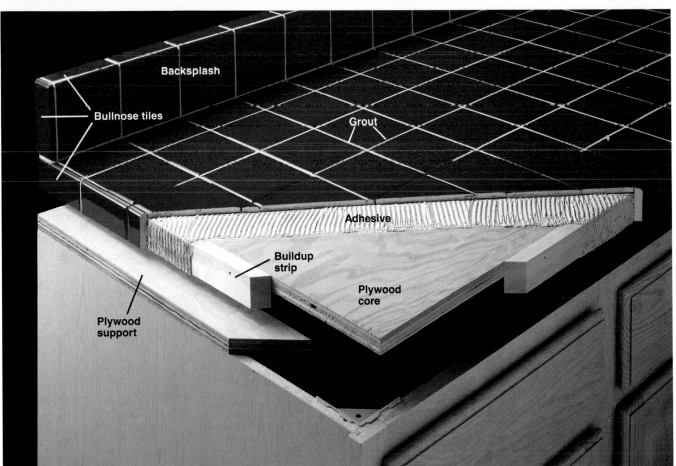

Backsplash

Bullnose tiles

Grout

Adhesive

Buildup strip

Plywood core

Plywood support

Ceramic tile countertop: Countertop core is ¾" exterior plywood cut to the same size as cabinet. Edges are built up with wood strips attached to outer edges of core. Tiles are set into place with adhesive. Grout fills gaps between tiles. Bullnose tiles, which have rounded edges, are used to cover edges of countertop and backsplash. Backsplash tiles can be installed over a separate plywood core, or directly to wall behind countertop. ¾" × 3" plywood supports are attached every 2 feet across base cabinet and around edges of cabinet.

Specialty tools & supplies include: sandpaper (A), denatured alcohol (B), latex grout additive (C), grout (D), silicone caulk (E), silicone sealer (F), carpenter's glue (G), latex underlayment (H), tile adhesive (I), short 2 × 4 wrapped in scrap carpeting (J), tile cutter (K), plastic spacers (L), foam paint brush (M), mallet (N), finish nails (O), wallboard screws (P), tile sander (Q), tile nippers (R), notched trowel (S), grout float (T), scoring tool (U).

How to Build a Ceramic Tile Countertop

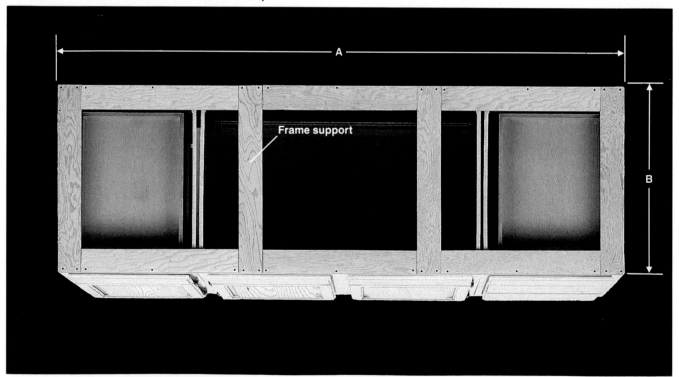

Frame support

1 Cut 3'' wide frame supports from ¾'' exterior plywood. Use 1¼'' wallboard screws or 4d common nails to attach supports every 24'' across cabinet, around perimeter, and next to cutout locations. From ¾'' exterior plywood, cut core to same size as cabinet unit (A × B), using a circular saw.

82

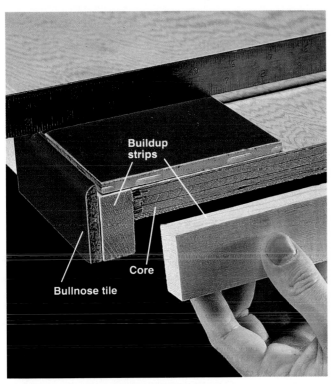

2 If countertop will have bullnose edge tiles, attach 1 × 2 buildup strips of pine or exterior plywood to exposed edges of countertop core, using carpenter's glue and 6d finish nails. Top of strip should be flush with top of core.

Option: for decorative wood edge, attach stained and sealed 1 × 2 hardwood strips to edge of core with carpenter's glue and finish nails. Top of edge strip should be flush with top surface of tile.

3 Position countertop core on cabinets and attach with sheetmetal or wallboard screws driven up through corner brackets inside cabinets. Screws should not be long enough to puncture top surface of core.

4 Use latex underlayment to fill any low spots and cracks in countertop core. Let underlayment dry, then sand smooth.

(continued next page)

5 To create a symmetrical tile layout, measure and mark the middle of the countertop core. Use a framing square to draw a layout line (A), perpendicular to the front edge of the core. Measure along line A from the front edge a distance equal to one full tile, and mark. Use the framing square to draw a second layout line (B) perpendicular to line A.

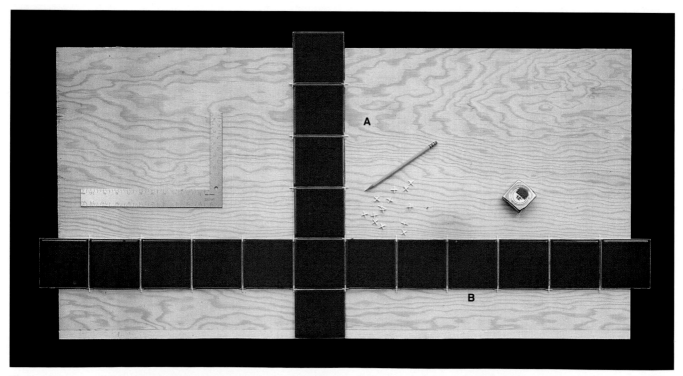

6 Dry-fit rows of tiles along layout lines. Use plastic spacers if tiles do not have self-spacing lugs. If dry-fit shows that layout is not pleasing, line A may be adjusted in either direction. Dry-fit all tiles, and mark cutting lines on any tiles that must be trimmed.

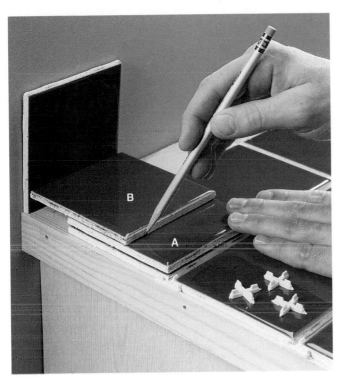

7 Mark border tiles for cutting. To allow for grout, place a tile upright against wall. Place a loose tile (A) over the last full tile. Place another tile (B) against upright tile, over tile A. Mark tile A and cut to fit border space.

8 To make straight cuts, place tile faceup in tile cutter. Adjust tool to proper width, then score a continuous line by pulling the cutting wheel firmly across face of tile.

9 Snap tile along scored line, as directed by tool manufacturer. Smooth the cut edges of tile with a tile sander.

10 For curved cuts, score a crosshatch outline of the cut with tile scoring tool. Use tile nippers to gradually break away small portions of tile until cutout is complete.

(continued next page)

11 Begin installation with edge tiles. Apply a thin layer of adhesive to edge of countertop and back of tile, using a notched trowel. Press tiles into place with a slight twist. Insert plastic spacers between tiles. (Self-spacing tiles require no plastic spacers.)

12 Remove dry-fit tiles next to layout lines. Spread adhesive along layout lines and install perpendicular rows of tiles. Use plastic spacers to maintain even spacing. Check alignment with framing square.

13 Install remaining tiles, working from layout line outward to ends. Work in small areas, about 18" square. Use denatured alcohol to remove any adhesive from face of tiles before it dries. For the backsplash, install a single row of bullnose tiles directly to wall, or build a separate backsplash core from ¾" plywood.

14 After each small area is installed, "set" the tiles. Wrap a short piece of 2 × 4 in scrap carpeting or a towel. Lay block against the tiles and tap lightly with a mallet or hammer. Remove plastic spacers with a toothpick.

15 Mix grout and latex additive. Apply grout with a rubber grout float. Use a sweeping motion to force grout into joints. Wipe away excess grout with a damp sponge. Let grout dry for 1 hour, then wipe away powdery haze. Let grout cure as directed by manufacturer before caulking and sealing.

16 Seal joints around backsplash with silicone caulk. Smooth bead with a wet finger. Wipe away excess caulk. Let caulk dry completely. Apply silicone sealer to countertop with a foam brush. Let dry, then apply second coat. Let dry, and buff with soft cloth.

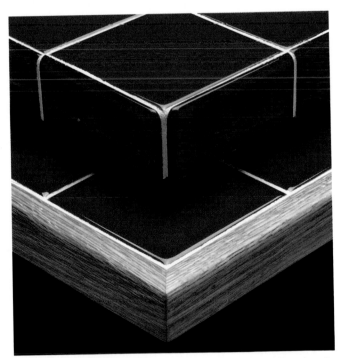

Edge treatments include rounded bullnose tiles (top) cut to fit edge, and hardwood edge (bottom) shaped with a router (page 78). Hardwood edges should be attached and finished before tile is installed. Protect hardwood with masking tape when grouting and sealing the tile job.

Solid-surface Countertops

Solid-surface materials, marketed under trade names such as Corian® and Avonite®, are manufactured from plastic resins blended with additives and are formed into sheets. They are made in solid colors or patterns that resemble marble or granite. For countertops, use ½" material. Use ¾" material for built-up edge treatments.

Solid-surface materials can be shaped with woodworking tools and carbide-tipped blades. To form corners and long countertops, sheets are welded together with color-matched joint adhesive.

Everything You Need:

Basic Hand Tools (page 62): tape measure, framing square, pencil, C-clamps, combination square, putty knife, caulk gun.

Basic Power Tools (page 63): circular saw with new carbide blade, plunge-cut router, jig saw with wood-cutting blade, orbital sander, belt sander.

Basic Materials: ½" and ¾" solid-surface material, ¾" × 4" plywood strips.

Specialty Tools & Supplies: photo, page opposite.

Countertops and molded sinks made from solid-surface materials are relatively expensive but are resistant to stains and scratches. If damaged, they usually can be repaired by simple sanding.

Specialty tools & supplies include: spring clamps (A), aluminum tape (B), denatured alcohol (C), carpenter's glue (D), joint adhesive (E), resilient construction or panel adhesive (F), silicone caulk (G), ½" dowels (H), 120-grit sanding belt (I), Scotch Brite® pad (J), 220-, 320-, 80-grit sandpaper (K), 4d common nails (L), wallboard screws (M), block plane (N), hot glue gun (O), scribing compass (P), ⅜" straight router bit (Q), corner rounding router bit (R).

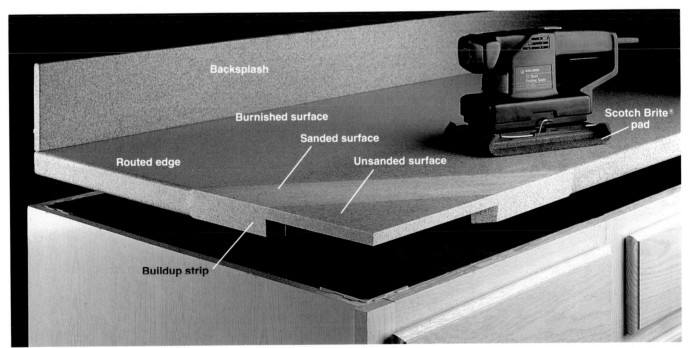

Backsplash
Burnished surface
Sanded surface
Routed edge
Unsanded surface
Scotch Brite® pad
Buildup strip

Solid-surface countertop: Countertop surface is made from ½" solid-surface material, shaped with woodworking tools. Countertop edges are built up with ¾" solid-surface strips attached with special joint adhesive. Edge is then shaped with a router. Surface is smoothed with sandpaper, and is burnished with a Scotch Brite® pad attached to the bottom of an orbital sander. Backsplash is attached to wall with panel adhesive and sealed with silicone caulk.

How to Build a Solid-surface Countertop

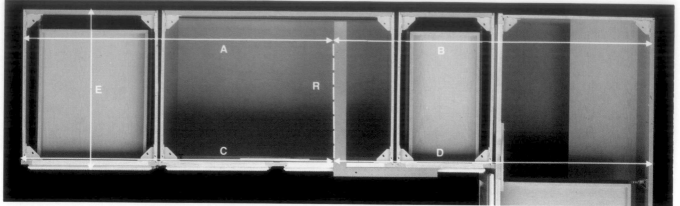

1 Measure along tops of base cabinets to determine the size of the countertop. Because wall corners may not be square, use a framing square to establish a reference line (R) near the middle of base cabinets, perpendicular to cabinet face. Take four measurements (A,B,C,D). Allow for overhangs by adding 1" to the length for each exposed end, and 1" to the width (E). If both ends will butt walls or appliances, subtract ¼" from the length to allow for the natural expansion and contraction of the material.

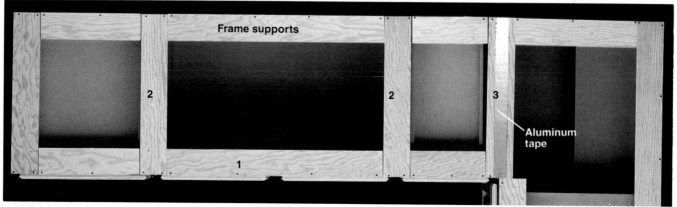

2 Distribute the weight of the solid-surface material by attaching ¾" × 4" plywood frame supports to top of base cabinet. Use carpenter's glue and 4d common nails or 1¼" wallboard screws to attach supports around perimeter (1), within 3" of sink or appliance cutouts (2), and where countertop sections will be joined together (3). At joint locations, cover frame supports with aluminum tape. Tape will prevent joint adhesive from bonding to the supports.

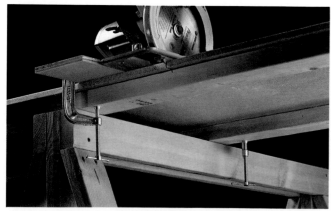

3 Transfer measurements from step 1 to the solid-surface material, using a framing square to establish a reference line. Support material on sawhorses with 2 × 4s. Cut with a circular saw and new carbide blade, using a clamped straightedge as guide.

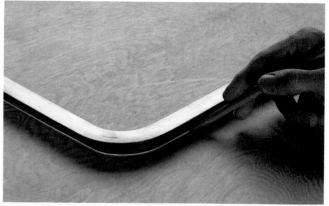

4 Make a plywood template as a guide for cutting sink or cooktop cutouts. Trace outline of cooktop frame or sink on plywood. Trace outline again at the correct location on the countertop material.

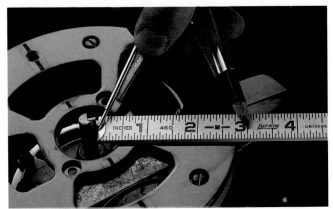

5 Mount ⅜" straight bit with carbide cutters in plunge-cut router. Set scribing compass equal to distance from cutting edge of bit to edge of router base. Add ¼" to this measurement to allow for the possible expansion and contraction of the solid-surface material.

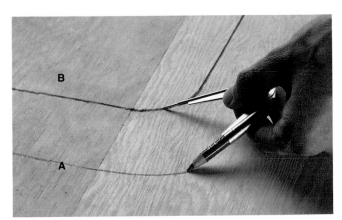

6 Use a scribing compass to draw a line (A) on plywood, parallel to the sink or cooktop outline (B). To create the template, cut along line A with a jig saw and fine-tooth wood-cutting blade.

7 Center plywood template around outline of sink on solid-surface material. Clamp into position. Make cutout with plunge router, keeping baseplate against inside edge of template. Support cutout area from below to prevent damage.

8 Round off sharp edges of cutout with an orbital sander. To prevent excessive heat buildup during cooking, wrap edges of cutout with aluminum tape.

9 Cut ¾" inch strips of ¾" solid-surface material to make edge buildups. Test-fit the length of the strips on top of the countertop. At corners, cut buildup strips so that one butts the other.

10 Clean strips with denatured alcohol. Mix joint adhesive. Apply thick bead of adhesive to top of buildup strips.

(continued next page)

11 Use spring clamps to attach buildup strips to bottom of countertop, flush with edge. Add adhesive to any cracks not filled. Puncture bubbles with toothpick. Do not wipe away excess adhesive. Let dry for one hour. Remove dried excess adhesive with a block plane.

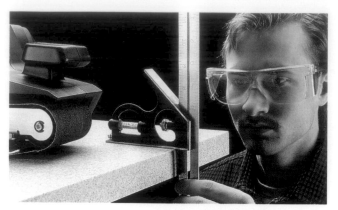

12 Smooth and straighten all edges with a belt sander and 120-grit belt. Check frequently with a square to make sure edges are exactly perpendicular. Square edges are essential when joining solid-surface pieces.

13 Position countertop pieces on cabinets, with ⅛" gap along walls, and ¹⁄₁₆" gap at joints between solid-surface pieces. Check for level. Shim countertop with aluminum tape, if needed.

14 At inside corner joints, tape a ½" wooden dowel tightly against corner. Cover bottom of corner with aluminum tape. Dowel helps mold joint adhesive into curved radius.

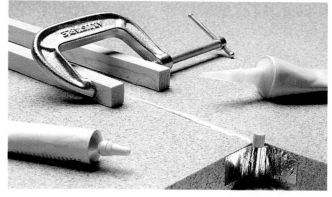

15 Attach wood strips near sides of joint with hot glue. Let dry. Mix joint adhesive and fill joint half full. Gently draw joint together with C-clamps on wood strips. Clamping too tightly will force all adhesive from joint. Puncture any bubbles with a toothpick. Add adhesive to areas not filled. Do not wipe away excess.

16 Let adhesive dry for one hour. Remove wood strips and hot glue with a putty knife. Remove corner dowel. Remove excess joint adhesive with block plane. Smooth joint with orbital sander and 220-grit paper. Sand until joint is barely visible.

17 Shape the exposed edges of countertop using a router and a corner rounding bit. Use a bit with a ball-bearing pilot and carbide cutters, and move router slowly.

18 Finish inside corners missed by router by hand-sanding with 80-grit, then 220-grit sandpaper.

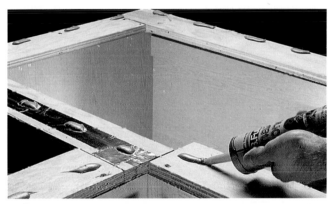

19 Carefully remove the countertop and apply 1" beads of resilient construction or panel adhesive every 6" on all countertop supports. Reposition countertop with ⅛" gap at walls. Press countertop lightly to bond it to cabinets. Let dry.

20 Cut 3½" to 4" backsplash from ½" or ¾" thick solid surface material. Sand out saw marks, and rout decorative edge, if desired. Apply 1" beads of panel adhesive to back of backsplash. Apply bead of silicone caulk to bottom edge.

21 Press backsplash tightly into place. Caulk gap between backsplash and wall. Smooth excess sealant with fingertip. Let caulk dry completely.

320-grit

Scotch Brite® pad

220-grit

22 Sand entire surface with orbital sander, first with 220-, then 320-grit paper. Burnish surface with Scotch Brite® pad attached to sander. Clean surface with denatured alcohol.

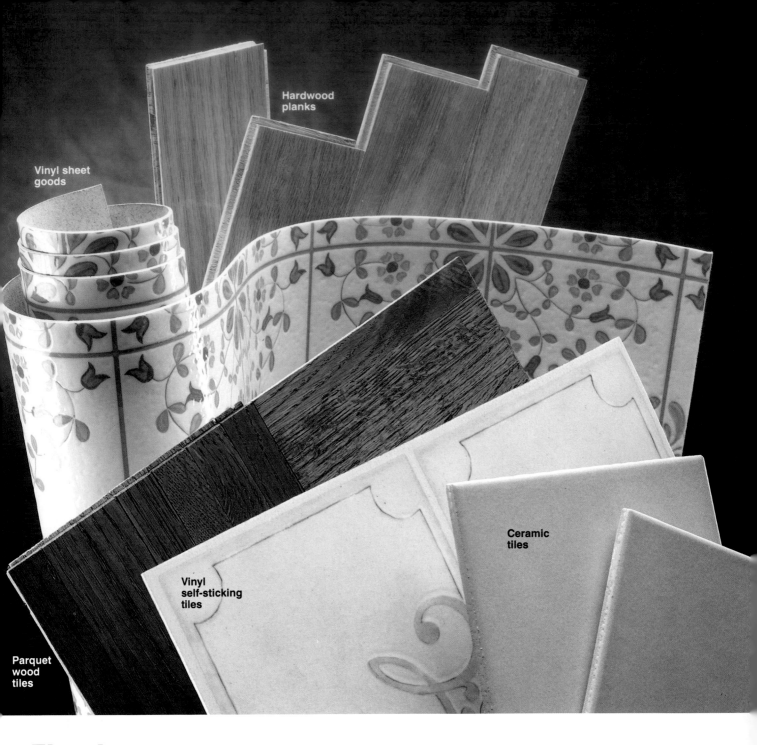

Vinyl sheet
goods

Hardwood
planks

Ceramic
tiles

Vinyl
self-sticking
tiles

Parquet
wood
tiles

Flooring

Give your kitchen a fresh look with new flooring. There are many floor covering products available that are rugged, beautiful, and designed especially for do-it-yourself installations.

Resilient vinyl floor coverings are good choices for kitchens. They resist moisture, and many of them are manufactured with a cushioned backing for added comfort. Resilient tile is one of the easiest floor surfaces to install. Resilient sheet goods can often be installed in a single piece, eliminating seams and preventing moisture from seeping through to the subfloor.

Hardwood flooring is available as strips, planks, or parquet tiles that come prefinished with coats of tough polyurethane. Prefinished wood flooring locks together with tongue-and-groove edges, and is installed over a troweled-on adhesive or thin sheets of foam.

Ceramic tile offers a wide variety of patterns, styles, and colors that can complement any room. Properly installed ceramic tile has timeless elegance, and is one of the most durable floor coverings available.

Planning for a New Floor Covering

New floor coverings can be installed directly over existing surfaces that are flat, level, and well bonded. Damaged, worn, or loose flooring can be removed (page 96), or repaired and covered with plywood underlayment (page 98) to provide a suitable base for new floor coverings.

In some instances, the addition of new flooring and plywood underlayment may interfere with the replacement of appliances (page 98). In these cases, the old flooring must be removed.

Carefully examine your old floor to determine what preparation, if any, must be completed before you install new flooring. Refer to the guidelines (right). Then measure your kitchen floor accurately to determine the quantity of new materials required.

Guidelines for Preparing Your Existing Floor

Resilient tile or sheet goods: New flooring can be installed directly over resilient goods. Cushioned or embossed resilient goods must be removed or covered with plywood underlayment.

Strip, plank, or parquet wood flooring: Roughen surface with sandpaper to remove gloss. Fill cracks with plastic filler and sand smooth. Damaged or warped wood floors should be sanded level and covered with plywood underlayment.

Ceramic tile: Roughen surface with 120-grit sandpaper to remove gloss. Level entire surface with latex underlayment, allow underlayment to dry, and sand smooth. New resilient sheet goods cannot be stapled to ceramic tile (page 108). Use flooring adhesive instead of staples.

Carpet: Always remove carpeting before installing new floor coverings.

Wood subfloors: Must be at least ¾" thick. Install ceramic tile over plywood subfloors that are at least 1⅛" total thickness.

Concrete slab subfloors: Consult a professional contractor to determine the condition of the slab.

How to Measure Your Kitchen

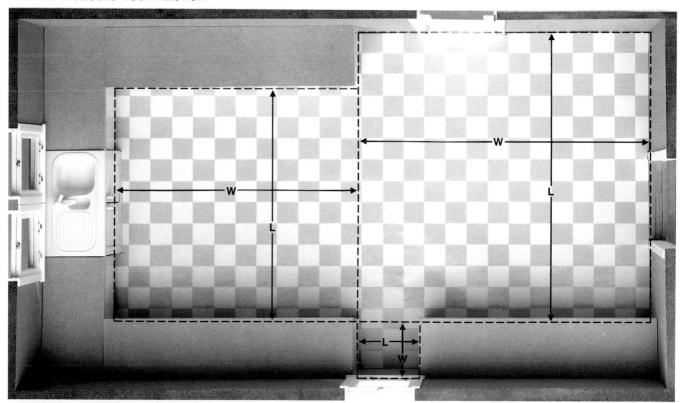

Determine total square footage by dividing the room into rectangles or squares. Include areas where moveable appliances are installed. Measure width and length of each area in inches, and multiply width times length. Divide that number by 144 to determine square footage. Add all areas together to estimate total square footage for the entire room.

Removing Flooring

Old flooring can be removed if the material has been badly damaged or if it is not well bonded to the subfloor. Refer to page 95.

Old resilient floor coverings that are embossed or cushioned should be removed or covered with plywood underlayment before installing new flooring.

Ceramic tile that is damaged or loose must be removed. Break the tiles with a hammer and pry up the pieces with a cold chisel (page 65).

> **Everything You Need:**
>
> Basic Hand Tools (page 62): eye protection, pry bar, pencil, tape measure, utility knife.
>
> Specialty Tools & Supplies: work gloves, heat gun, wallboard knife, floor scraper, rolling pin.

Rolling pin can be used to remove flooring after it is cut into strips.

How to Remove Resilient Tiles

1 Soften flooring adhesive by warming tiles with a heat gun. Remember to wear eye protection and gloves.

2 Pry up tiles with a wallboard knife. Use the knife to scrape off old adhesive.

3 Stubborn adhesive can be removed using a long-handled floor scraper. Floor scrapers can be rented.

How to Remove Resilient Sheet Goods

1 Remove base shoe and baseboards with a pry bar and wallboard knife. Wallboard knife protects wall surfaces. Number each piece and save for reinstallation.

2 Use a utility knife to cut old flooring into 10" wide strips.

3 For easy removal, peel up an edge of the cut flooring and wrap it around a rolling pin.

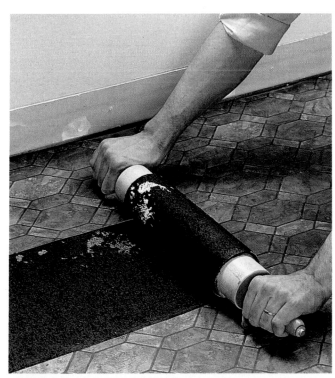

4 Gather up each strip of flooring by rolling the pin smoothly along cut lines. Cushioned sheet goods may separate and leave the felt backing still attached to the subfloor.

5 Remove felt backing entirely. Moisten glued felt with soapy water and remove with floor scraper or wallboard knife.

Installing Underlayment

Cover your kitchen floor with plywood underlayment to make sure your new flooring is installed over a flat, level surface. Refer to the guidelines on page 95.

Use high quality ¼" lauan plywood for underlayment. Lauan plywood provides a flat, uniform surface that makes an ideal underlayment. It comes in 4' × 8' sheets and is available in varying grades at most lumber or home building supply centers. Be certain to buy high-grade lauan. Cheaper grades can delaminate and void the sheet vinyl manufacturer's warranty.

Examine the old floor thoroughly. Nail down any loose flooring with 6d ring-shank nails. Set all nail heads below flooring surface. Fill cracks or holes with plastic filler.

> **Everything You Need:**
>
> Basic Hand Tools (page 62): tape measure, hand saw, hammer.
>
> Basic Power Tools (page 63): circular saw or jig saw with wood-cutting blade.
>
> Basic Materials: ¼" lauan plywood underlayment.
>
> Specialty Tools & Supplies: photo, below.

How to Install Plywood Underlayment

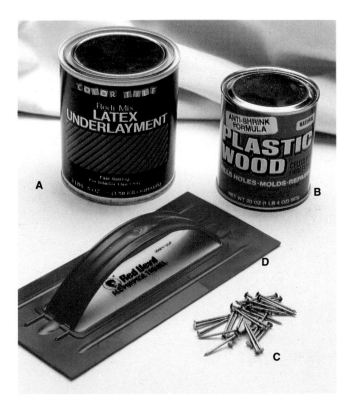

Specialty tools & supplies include: latex underlayment (A), plastic filler (B), 6d ring-shank nails (C), flat trowel (D).

1 Remove moveable appliances, like dishwashers or refrigerators. These areas will receive underlayment and new flooring. Make sure finished height of new floor will allow appliances to be replaced. Countertop may need to be shimmed up, or old flooring removed, to allow appliances to fit.

2 Undercut door casings with a hand saw to allow new flooring to slide under casing. Use a scrap of underlayment and piece of new flooring as a spacing guide when cutting.

3 Inspect subfloor for low spots. Fill low areas with latex underlayment. Let underlayment dry, then sand smooth.

4 Install plywood underlayment along longest wall or base cabinet run. Secure with 6d ring-shank nails driven every 8" along edge and spaced every 8" throughout sheet.

5 Cover remaining areas, staggering plywood seams. Leave 1/8" between underlayment sheets for expansion. Fill gaps and holes with nonshrinking plastic filler. Let dry and sand smooth.

Installing Resilient Vinyl or Wood Floor Tiles

Resilient vinyl tiles are easy to install. Many styles are available with self-sticking adhesive backs, and are made for do-it-yourself projects. Some resilient tiles and most wood parquet tiles should be set in flooring adhesive. Wood parquet tiles lock together with tongue-and-groove edges.

Establish perpendicular layout lines to guide your tile installation. Tiles should be "dry-fit" prior to gluing to make sure the finished pattern is pleasing. Begin installation at the center of the room and work toward the walls.

Everything You Need:

Basic Hand Tools (page 62): tape measure, framing square, utility knife.

Basic Power Tools (page 63): jig saw with wood-cutting blade.

Basic Materials: floor tiles.

Specialty Tools & Supplies: photo, right.

Specialty tools & supplies include: wood tile adhesive (A), adhesive remover (B), resilient tile adhesive (C), notched spreader (D), J-roller (E), notched trowel (F), flooring knife (G).

How to Establish Layout Lines for Tile Installations

1 Establish a layout line by measuring opposite sides of the room and marking the center of each side. Snap a chalk line between the marks.

2 Measure and mark the center of the chalk line. From this point, use a framing square to establish a second line perpendicular to the first. Snap second layout line across the room.

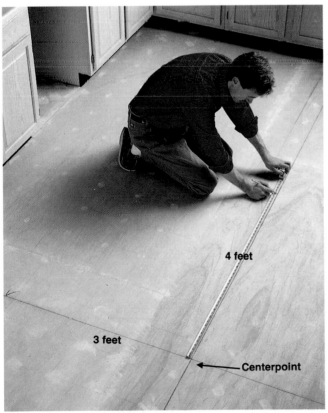

3 Check for squareness with a "carpenter's triangle." Measure and mark one layout line 3' from the centerpoint. Measure and mark the perpendicular layout line 4' from the centerpoint.

4 Measure distance between marks. If layout lines are perpendicular, the distance will be exactly 5'.

Self-sticking tiles bond instantly. Peel off backing, and position each tile with care. Misaligned tiles should be softened with a heat gun or iron and removed.

Make cardboard templates the same size as tile. Use templates to test-fit cuts at wall corners or around pipes and posts. Trace template outline on tile for cutting.

Bond flooring by applying pressure with a floor roller or rolling pin.

Use notched trowel to spread flooring adhesive according to manufacturer's directions. Take care not to cover layout lines with adhesive.

Wipe up adhesive that seeps between tile joints immediately. Use a solvent recommended by flooring adhesive manufacturer.

Use scrap plywood pieces for kneeling on set tiles. Plywood distributes weight to prevent tiles from shifting.

How to Install Tiles

1 Dry-fit tiles along layout lines in both directions. Make sure that the finished layout is pleasing.

2 Adjust layout, if necessary. Snap a new line parallel to the original. Dry-fit tiles to new layout line.

New layout line

Old layout line

3 Begin laying tiles at the centerpoint. Apply tiles to one quadrant of floor, laying tiles in sequence shown. Repeat for other quadrants.

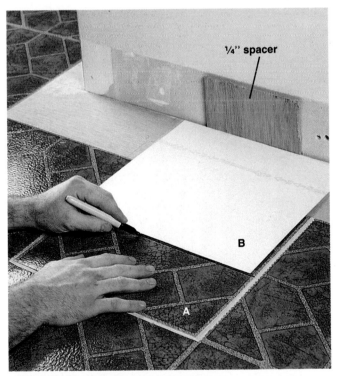

¼" spacer

B

A

4 Mark border tiles for cutting. To allow for expansion and contraction of the subfloor, leave a ¼" gap at walls. Place a ¼" spacer upright against wall. Place a loose tile (A) directly over the last full tile. Place another tile (B) against spacer, over tile A. Mark tile A as shown, and cut. Cut resilient tile with a utility knife; wood parquet with a jig saw.

Installing Resilient Sheet Goods

Resilient sheet goods are made of vinyl and are manufactured in six- or twelve-foot widths. Use a floor plan of your kitchen to determine if your sheet goods can be installed without seams. Large kitchens may require that pieces of flooring be joined together, so try to plan any seams for inconspicuous areas.

To eliminate cutting errors, create a template of your kitchen with heavy paper. A paper template allows you to trace an accurate outline of your kitchen onto the new flooring. Find a large, level area to lay the flooring completely flat.

Everything You Need:

Basic Hand Tools (page 62): utility knife, framing square.

Basic Materials: heavy butcher's paper, masking tape, resilient sheet goods, compass.

Specialty Tools & Supplies: photo, page 106.

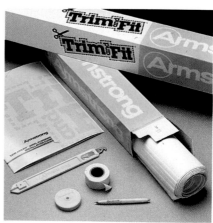

Template kits are offered by some flooring manufacturers. Many manufacturers will warrant the do-it-yourself installation of their sheet goods when their kits are used.

How to Make a Cutting Template

1 Use sheets of heavy butcher's or builder's paper. Place the edges of paper against walls, leaving 1/8" margin. Cut triangular holes in paper with a utility knife. Fasten the template to the floor by placing masking tape over the holes.

2 Follow the outline of the room, working with one sheet of paper at a time. Overlap edges of adjoining sheets 2" and tape together.

3 To fit template around pipes, tape sheets of paper on either side. Measure distance from wall to center of pipe, using a framing or combination square, and subtract 1/8".

4 Transfer measurement to a separate piece of paper. Use a compass to draw the pipe diameter onto the paper, and cut hole with scissors or utility knife. Cut a slit from edge of paper to hole.

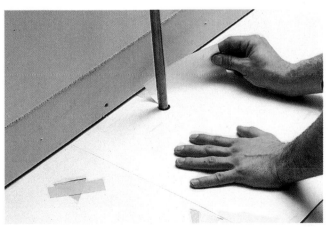

5 Fit hole cutout around pipe. Tape the hole template to adjoining sheets.

6 When completed, roll or loosely fold the paper template for carrying. Get a helper to lay sheet goods out on a flat, level area.

Specialty tools & supplies include: flooring adhesives (A), straightedge (B), rolling pin (C), notched trowel (D), J-roller (E), flooring knife (F), stapler (G).

How to Install Resilient Sheet Goods

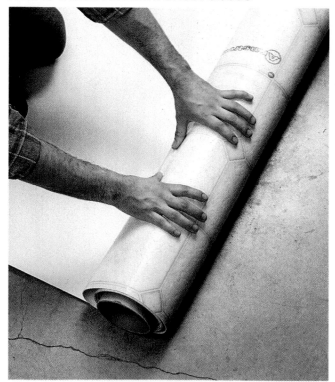

1 Unroll flooring on any large, flat, clean surface. To prevent wrinkles, sheet goods come from manufacturer rolled with the pattern side out. Unroll the sheet and turn it pattern side up for marking.

For two-piece installations, overlap edges of sheets at least 2". Plan seams to fall along pattern lines or simulated grout joint. Align sheets so that pattern matches, and tape sheets together.

2 Position paper template on sheet goods and tape into place. Trace outline of template onto flooring with a felt-tipped pen.

3 Remove template. Cut sheet goods with a sharp flooring knife, or a utility knife with a new blade.

4 Cut holes for pipes or posts using a flooring knife or utility knife. Then cut a slit from hole to the nearest edge of sheet goods. Make cuts along pattern lines, if possible.

5 Roll up flooring loosely and transfer to kitchen. Do not fold flooring. Unroll and position sheet goods carefully. Slide edges beneath undercut door casings (page 99).

(continued next page)

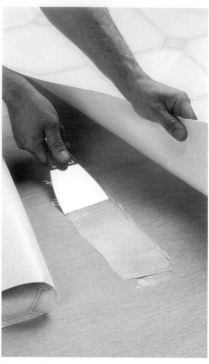

6 Cut seams for two-piece installations, using a straightedge as a guide. Hold straightedge tightly against flooring, and cut along pattern lines through both pieces of vinyl flooring.

7 Remove both pieces of scrap flooring. The sheet goods now will be pattern-matched.

8 Fold back edges of seam and apply a 3" band of flooring adhesive to the subfloor with notched trowel.

9 Lay seam edges one at a time into adhesive. Make sure seam is tight. Bond seam edges with a J-roller.

10 Fasten outer edges of sheet goods to wooden subfloor with ⅜" staples driven every 3". Make sure staples will be covered by base molding.

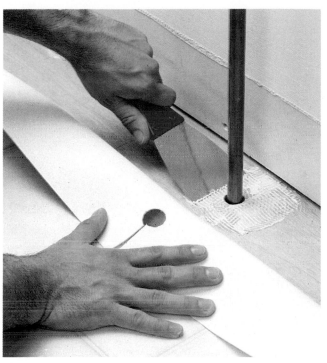

11 At pipes or posts, apply seam adhesive underneath flooring cuts. Bond with J-roller.

Bond flooring to concrete or other hard surfaces by applying 3" band of flooring adhesive instead of staples around edges.

How to Glue Full-spread Sheet Goods

1 Some kinds of sheet goods require a full spread of adhesive under the flooring. Glue one-half of sheet at a time. Dry-fit sheet goods, then fold back half of sheet and apply adhesive to floor with a notched trowel.

2 Lay flooring on adhesive, then repeat procedure for other half of sheet. Bond sheet goods with a rolling pin or J-roller.

Installing Prefinished Hardwood Flooring

Install prefinished hardwood flooring for a warm and inviting look in your kitchen, and for comfort underfoot. Hardwood flooring is manufactured as strips 2" to 4" wide, or planks more than 4" wide. Prefinished flooring locks together with tongue-and-groove edges, and comes stained and finished with coats of tough polyurethane.

Hardwood flooring is usually installed over a troweled-on adhesive, but some types are glued tongue-to-groove and "floated" on thin sheets of foam underlayment. Hardwood strips and planks can be laid on any smooth, dry, and level subfloor.

Everything You Need:

Basic Hand Tools (page 62): tape measure, chalk line.

Basic Power Tools (page 63): jig saw with wood-cutting blade.

Basic Materials: prefinished hardwood flooring, cardboard, masking tape.

Specialty Tools & Supplies: photo, right.

Specialty tools & supplies include: floor roller (A), flooring adhesive (B), carpenter's glue (C), notched trowel (D), mallet (E), chalk line (F).

How to Install Glue-down Hardwood Flooring

1 Establish a straight layout line for hardwood flooring installation. Snap a chalk line parallel to the longest wall, about 30" from the wall. Kneel in this space to begin flooring installation.

2 Apply adhesive to subfloor with a notched trowel, according to manufacturer's directions. Take care not to cover layout line with adhesive. Work away from 30" space.

(continued next page)

3 Apply carpenter's glue to grooved end of each piece of flooring just before installing. Glue helps flooring joints stay tight. Do not apply glue to long edge of boards.

4 Install starter row of flooring with edge of tongue directly over chalkline. Make sure end joints are tight, then wipe up any excess carpenter's glue immediately. At walls, leave a ½" margin to allow for seasonal expansion of the wood. This gap will be covered by the baseboard and base shoe.

5 For succeeding rows, insert tongue into groove of preceding row, and pivot flooring down into adhesive. Gently slide tongue-and-groove ends together.

6 Use a mallet and a scrap of flooring to gently tap boards into position. All joints should fit tightly.

7 Use a cardboard template to fit boards in irregular areas. Cut cardboard to match space, and allow for expansion gap next to wall. Trace template outline on board, then cut to fit with a jig saw.

8 Bond flooring by applying pressure with a heavy flooring roller. Roll flooring within three hours of adhesive application. Roller can be borrowed or rented from flooring distributor.

How to Install a Floating Plank Floor

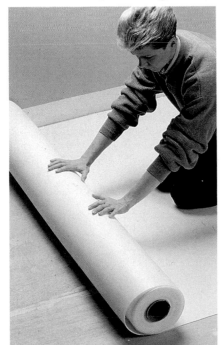

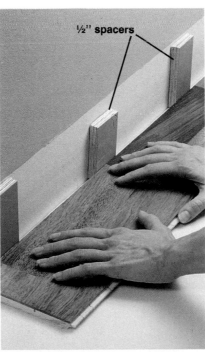

1 Roll out foam backing and cut to fit room. Secure joints with masking tape.

2 Begin installation at longest kitchen wall. Use ½" spacers to provide gap for seasonal expansion of flooring.

3 Join planks by applying carpenter's glue to tongues of planks. Complete installation as for glue-down flooring (steps 5 to 7).

Installing Ceramic Floor Tile

Ceramic floor tile is available in many styles, colors, and patterns. Glazed tile has a hard surface layer of color and may be glossy, matte, or textured. Unglazed tile, often called quarry tile, has color throughout its thickness. Quarry tile must be protected with a masonry sealer after installation.

Ceramic floor tiles can be installed over existing floor coverings that are flat and well bonded to the subfloor. Refer to the guidelines on page 95. Note that ceramic tile should be installed over subfloors no less than 1⅛" total thickness. Thinner subfloors may flex, causing the tiles to break or the grout to crack. Do not install ceramic floor tiles over particleboard subfloors. If necessary, hire a professional contractor for an evaluation of your subfloor.

Lay out ceramic floor tiles using the same technique as used for resilient or wood parquet tiles (pages 100 to 103). Dry-fit the tiles prior to installation, to make sure the finished pattern is pleasing.

Everything You Need:

Basic Hand Tools (page 62): pencil.

Basic Materials: ceramic tiles, plastic grout spacers.

Specialty Tools & Supplies: photo, page opposite.

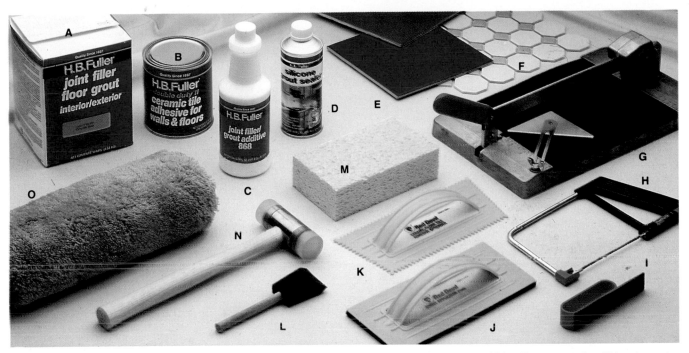

Specialty tools & supplies include: grout (A), adhesive (B), latex grout additive (C), silicone sealer (D), glazed tile (E), mosaic tile (F), tile cutter (G), tile saw (H), tile sander (I), grout float (J), notched trowel (K), foam brush (L), sponge (M), mallet (N), 2 × 4 wrapped in scrap carpeting (O).

How to Install Ceramic Floor Tile

1 Prepare the floor and draw perpendicular guidelines through centerpoint of floor (pages 98 to 102). Dry-fit tiles so that finished layout will be pleasing to the eye.

2 Apply adhesive to floor according to manufacturer's directions. Begin at centerpoint. Use a notched trowel, and take care not to cover layout lines.

3 Begin laying tiles at centerpoint, placing edges against layout lines. Use plastic spacers to maintain even grout lines between tiles.

(continued next page)

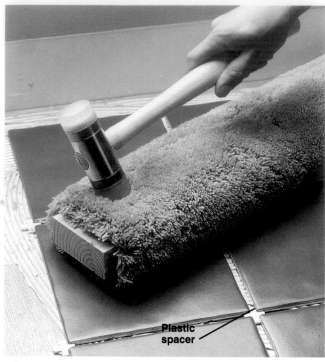

4 Wrap a short piece of 2 × 4 in scrap carpeting or a towel. Lay 2 × 4 against tiles and tap lightly with mallet to set tiles in adhesive. Remove plastic spacers with a toothpick.

5 Mark border tiles for cutting. To allow space for grout, place a scrap tile upright against wall. Place a loose tile (A) directly over last full tile. Place another tile (B) against upright tile, over tile A. Mark tile A and cut to fit border space.

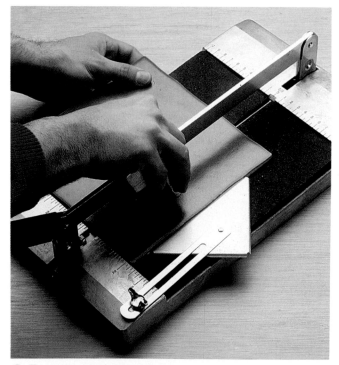

6 To make straight cuts, place tile faceup in tile cutter. Adjust tool to proper width, then score a continuous line by pulling cutting wheel across tile face. Snap tile along scored line. Smooth rough edge of cut tile with a tile sander.

7 Use a cardboard template to fit tiles in irregular areas. Cut cardboard to match area, and allow for grout lines. Trace template outline on tile, then cut to fit.

8 Secure tile with vise or clamps for cutting irregular shapes. Jaws of vise should be faced with rubber or wood to prevent scratches. Cut along outline with a tile saw. Smooth rough edges with a tile sander.

9 Mix grout and latex additive according to manufacturer's directions. Apply grout to floor with a rubber float. Use a sweeping motion to force grout into joints.

10 Wipe away excess grout with a damp sponge. Let grout dry slightly, then wipe away powdery haze. Let grout cure as directed by manufacturer.

11 Apply silicone sealer to floor with a foam brush or squeegee. Let dry, then apply a second coat.

Cabinets

Cabinets determine how a kitchen looks and functions. Cabinets should provide adequate storage, and have a pleasing appearance that harmonizes with other elements in the kitchen and home.

Paint existing cabinets to give your entire kitchen new life at minimum cost. Wood, metal, and previously painted cabinets may be painted any color. Do not paint plastic laminate.

Reface cabinets to create a dramatic change in style. Refacing kits include new cabinet doors, drawer fronts, and matching veneer for covering face frames and cabinet ends. All types of cabinets can be refaced.

Install new cabinets to transform a kitchen completely. New cabinets come in a wide range of styles and colors, and most manufacturers offer a variety of accessories that can increase storage efficiency.

Several companies make modular cabinets designed especially for do-it-yourself installations. Modular cabinets have finished end panels on both sides, and can be arranged to fit any kitchen layout.

Cabinet Options

Paint cabinets (pages 120 to 121) to add new life to your kitchen at a modest price.

Reface cabinets (pages 122 to 125) by replacing doors and drawer fronts, and applying new veneer to cabinet sides and face frames. Refacing costs substantially less than installing all-new cabinets.

Install new cabinets (pages 126 to 141) to transform a kitchen completely. Several styles of cabinets are designed especially for do-it-yourself installation.

Painting Cabinets

Paint cabinets to renew your kitchen quickly and inexpensively. Cabinets receive heavy use and are frequently scrubbed, so paint them with heavy-duty gloss enamel. Enamel paint is more durable than flat wall paint. Most jobs will require two coats of paint. Sand surfaces lightly between coats.

Use natural bristle paint brushes with alkyd paints, synthetic bristle brushes with latex.

Varnished cabinets can be painted if the surface is properly prepared. Use liquid deglosser to dull the shine, then prime all surfaces. Alkyd paints work best for painting varnished cabinets.

Everything You Need:

Basic Hand Tools (page 62): screwdriver.

Basic Materials: gloss enamel paint.

Specialty Tools & Supplies: photo, below.

Specialty tools & supplies include: work light (A), paint pan (B), paint remover (C), primer/sealer (D), tapered sash brush (E), trim brush (F), scraper (G), sandpaper (H), paint rollers (I).

How to Paint Cabinets

1 Empty cabinets. Remove doors, drawers, removable shelves, and all hardware. If hardware is to be repainted, strip old paint by soaking hardware in paint remover.

2 Wash cabinets with mild detergent. Scrape loose paint. Sand all surfaces. Wipe away sanding dust and prime all bare wood with sealer.

3 Paint interiors first, in this order: 1) back walls, 2) tops, 3) sides, 4) bottoms. Paint bottoms, tops, and edges of shelves last.

4 Paint large outside surfaces using a short-nap roller. Work from the top down.

5 Paint both sides of doors, beginning with inner surfaces. With panel doors, paint in this order: 1) recessed panels, 2) horizontal rails, 3) vertical stiles.

6 Paint drawer fronts last. Let doors and drawers dry several days, then install hardware and hang doors.

Refacing Cabinets

Reface existing kitchen cabinets for a dramatic change in style. Refacing kits include new doors, drawer fronts, and veneer for resurfacing cabinet face frames and sides. Replacement hardware can also be ordered.

Everything You Need:

Basic Hand Tools (page 62): utility knife, straight-edge, combination square, handsaw.

Basic Power Tools (page 63): drill, cordless screwdriver.

Basic Materials: refacing kit, stain and polyurethane finish (for unfinished refacing materials), cabinet hardware.

Specialty Tools & Supplies: wallcovering roller, paint scraper, 100- and 150-grit sandpaper.

How to Reface Cabinets

1 Remove the old doors, hinges, catches, and other hardware. Paint interior of cabinets, if desired (pages 120 to 121).

2 Scrape any loose or peeling finish. Fill any holes and chips with latex wood patch. Let dry, then lightly sand cabinet sides, faces, and edges with 150-grit sandpaper.

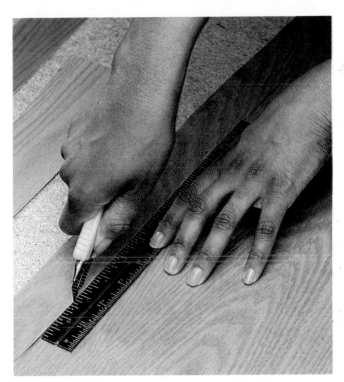

3 Remove veneer from package and lay flat on a smooth surface. Measure each surface to be covered, and add ¼" for overlap. Cut veneer pieces with utility knife and straightedge.

4 Apply veneer to vertical frame members first. Peel veneer backing off to reveal one corner of adhesive. Align veneer and press lightly to adhere corner. Gradually remove the backing, and smooth out air bubbles with fingertips. Trim excess veneer with a utility knife.

5 Apply veneer to horizontal frame members, overlapping vertical frame member. Trim excess with utility knife, using a straightedge as a guide. Apply veneer to cabinet sides, and trim excess with a utility knife.

(continued next page)

6 Bond veneer by rolling entire surface with a wall-covering roller.

7 Stain the new doors and drawer fronts, if they are unfinished. Stain unfinished veneer to match. Apply three coats of polyurethane finish, sanding lightly with 150-grit sandpaper between coats.

8 Lock a combination square at 2" mark. Use square to position hinges an equal distance from top and bottom of door. Use a finish nail or awl to mark screw locations.

9 Drill pilot holes and attach the hinges with screws. Mount knobs, handles, and catches. A cordless screwdriver speeds up this job.

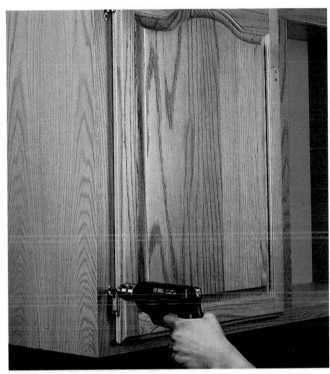

10 Attach cabinet doors to frames. Make sure doors overlap openings by an equal amount on all sides. Allow ⅛" gap between doors that cover a single opening.

11 Saw off all overhanging edges of existing solid (one-piece) drawer fronts. If drawer fronts are two-piece, remove screws and discard decorative face panel.

12 Attach new fronts by drilling pilot holes and driving screws through inside of drawers into new drawer fronts. Make sure drawer fronts overlap drawers by an equal margin on all sides.

False drawer front

13 Attach false drawer fronts on sink and cooktop cabinets by cutting wood blocks to span the drawer openings. Place blocks across openings on inside of cabinets. Fasten by driving screws through wood blocks into false fronts.

Framed cabinets have openings that are completely surrounded by face frames made of vertical **stiles** and horizontal **rails** . They give kitchens a traditional look.

Frameless cabinets, sometimes called "European-style," are more contemporary. Because they have no face frames, frameless cabinets offer slightly more storage space than framed cabinets.

Hinges on framed cabinets are screwed directly to the face frames. Better cabinets have adjustable hinges that allow door realignment.

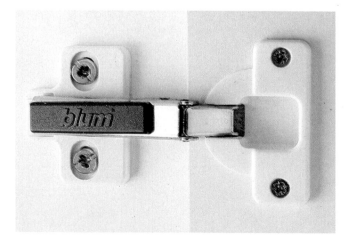

Hinges on frameless cabinets are screwed directly to the inside of the cabinet, eliminating the need for face frames. Hinges are hidden, providing a cleaner look.

Selecting New Cabinets

Kitchen cabinets come in a wide array of shapes and finishes, but their basic construction is similar. Different styles of doors, drawer fronts, and hardware give cabinets their individual character and personality.

Framed cabinets have cabinet openings that are completely surrounded by face frames, and door hinges are attached directly to the frames. Framed cabinets typically have a traditional look.

Frameless cabinets (also called "European-style") have no face frames. Special "invisible" hinges attach to the inside walls of the cabinet. The doors and drawers on frameless cabinets cover the entire unit, providing contemporary styling and slightly more storage space.

Specification booklet lists all dimensions of cabinets and trim pieces. Draw a kitchen floor plan on graph paper, and use catalog when sketching cabinet layout.

Modular cabinets have finished panels on both sides, and can be arranged in a variety of ways to fit any kitchen layout. Modular cabinet doors can be reversed to open from either left or right. They are especially suited to do-it-yourself installations.

All cabinet manufacturers offer a selection of specialty cabinets, storage accessories, and decorative trim. Check manufacturers' product-line catalogs for complete listings of available cabinets and accessories.

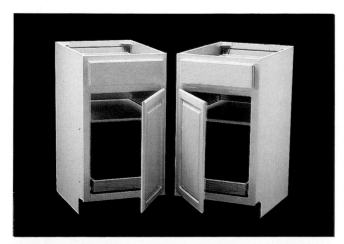

Modular cabinets have finished panels on both sides. Doors can be reversed to open from either left or right. Modular cabinets can be arranged to fit any kitchen layout.

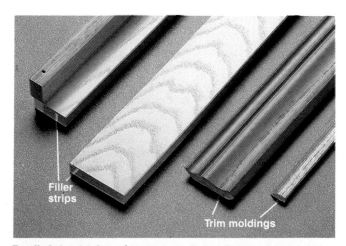

Prefinished trim pieces match the finish of modular cabinets. Filler strips are used in spaces between cabinets, or between a cabinet and wall or appliance. Small trim moldings cover gaps between cabinet edges and walls.

Removing Trim & Old Cabinets

Old cabinets can be salvaged if they are modular units that were installed with screws. Built-in cabinets should be cut into pieces and discarded.

Everything You Need:

Basic Hand Tools (page 62): pry bar, putty knife.

Basic Power Tools (page 63): cordless screwdriver.

Specialty Tools: reciprocating saw.

How to Remove Trim

Remove trim moldings at edges and tops of cabinets with a flat pry bar or putty knife.

Remove vinyl base trim. Work a pry bar or putty knife underneath and peel off the vinyl.

Remove baseboards and base shoe moldings with a pry bar. Protect wall surfaces with scraps of wood.

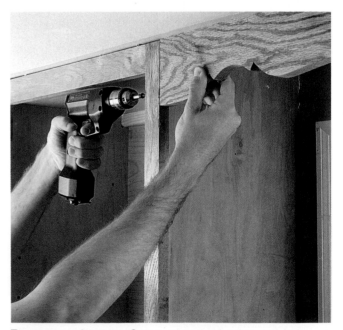

Remove valances. Some are attached to cabinets or soffits with screws. Others are nailed and must be pried loose.

How to Remove Cabinets

1 Remove doors and drawers to make it easier to get at interior spaces. You may need to scrape away old paint to expose hinge screws.

2 At back of cabinets, remove any screws holding cabinet to wall. Cabinets can be removed as a group, or can be disassembled.

3 Detach individual cabinets by removing screws that hold face frames together.

Built-in cabinets are usually not salvageable. Cut them into manageable pieces with a reciprocating saw, or take them apart piece by piece with a hammer and pry bar.

Preparing for New Cabinets

Sanded high area

Stud finder

Filled-in low area

Installing new cabinets is easiest if the kitchen is completely empty. Disconnect the plumbing and wiring, and temporarily remove the appliances. To remove old cabinets, see page 129. If the new kitchen will require plumbing or electrical changes, now is the time to have this work done. If the kitchen flooring is to be replaced, finish the work before beginning layout and installation of cabinets.

Cabinets must be installed plumb and level. Using a level as a guide, draw reference lines on the walls to indicate cabinet locations. If the kitchen floor is uneven, find the highest point of the floor area that will be covered by base cabinets. Measure up from this point to draw the reference lines.

Everything You Need:

Basic Hand Tools (page 62): pry bar, putty knife, screwdriver, straightedge, level, marking pencil, tape measure.

Basic Power Tools (page 63): cordless screwdriver.

Basic Materials: 1 × 3 boards, straight six-to eight-foot-long 2 × 4.

Specialty Tools & Supplies: wallboard compound, trowel, stud finder, 2½" wallboard screws.

30"

Stud locations

1 × 3
ledger

84"

Reference
line

34½"

1 Find high and low spots on wall surfaces, using a long, straight 2 × 4. Sand down any high spots.

2 Fill in low spots of wall. Apply wallboard taping compound with a trowel. Let dry, and sand lightly.

3 Locate and mark wall studs, using an electronic stud finder. Cabinets will be hung by driving screws into the studs through the back of the cabinets.

High point

4 Find high point along the floor area that will be covered by base cabinets. Place a level on a long, straight 2 × 4, and move board across floor to determine if floor is uneven. Mark wall at the high point.

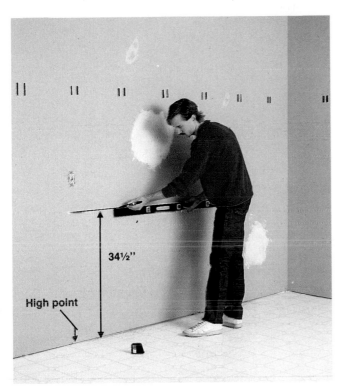

5 Measure up 34½" from the high-point mark. Use a level to mark a reference line on walls. Base cabinets will be installed with top edges flush against this line.

6 Measure up 84" from the high-point mark and draw a second reference line. Wall cabinets will be installed with top edges flush against this line.

7 Measure down 30" from wall-cabinet reference line and draw another level line where bottom of cabinets will be. Temporary ledgers will be installed against this line.

8 Install 1 × 3 temporary ledgers with top edge flush against the reference line. Attach ledgers with 2½" wallboard screws driven into every other wall stud. Mark stud locations on ledgers. Cabinets will rest temporarily on ledgers during installation.

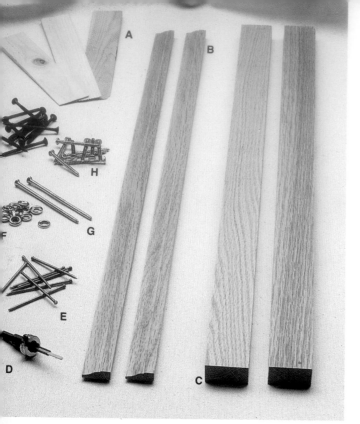

Specialty tools & supplies include: wood shims (A), trim moldings (B), filler strips (C), No. 9 counterbore drill bit (D), 6d finish nails (E), finish washers (F), No. 10 gauge 4'' wood screws (G), No. 8 gauge 2½'' sheetmetal screws (H), 3'' wallboard screws (I).

Installing Cabinets

Cabinets must be firmly anchored to wall studs, and must be exactly plumb and level, so that the doors and drawers operate smoothly. Number each cabinet and mark its position on the wall. Remove the cabinet doors and drawers, and number them so they can be easily replaced after the cabinets are installed.

Begin with the corner cabinets, making sure they are installed plumb and level. Adjacent cabinets are easily aligned once the corner cabinets have been correctly positioned.

Everything You Need:

Basic Hand Tools (page 62): handscrew clamps, level, hammer, utility knife, nail set, stepladder.

Basic Power Tools (page 63): drill with ³⁄₁₆'' twist bit, cordless screwdriver, jig saw with wood-cutting blade.

Basic Materials: cabinets, trim molding, toe-kick molding, filler strips, valance.

Specialty Tools & Supplies: photo, left.

How to Fit Blind Corner Cabinet

Before installation, test-fit corner and adjoining cabinets to make sure doors and handles do not interfere with each other. If necessary, increase the clearance by pulling the blind cabinet away from side wall by no more than 4''. To maintain even spacing between edges of doors and cabinet corner (A, B), cut a filler strip and attach it to the adjoining cabinet. Measure distance (C) as a reference when positioning blind cabinet against wall.

How to Install Wall Cabinets

1 Position corner cabinet on ledger. Drill ³⁄₁₆" pilot holes into studs through hanging strips at rear of cabinet. Attach to wall with 2½" sheetmetal screws. Do not tighten fully until all cabinets are hung.

2 Attach filler strip to adjoining cabinet, if needed (see page opposite). Clamp filler in place, and drill pilot holes through cabinet face frame near hinge locations, using a counterbore bit. Attach filler to cabinet with 2½" sheetmetal screws.

3 Position adjoining cabinet on ledger, tight against blind corner cabinet. Check face frame for plumb. Drill ³⁄₁₆" pilot holes into wall studs through hanging strips in rear of cabinet. Attach cabinet with 2½" sheet-metal screws. Do not tighten wall screws fully until all cabinets are hung.

4 Clamp corner cabinet and adjoining cabinet together at the top and bottom. Handscrew clamps will not damage wood face frames.

(continued next page)

5 Attach blind corner cabinet to adjoining cabinet. From inside corner cabinet, drill pilot holes through face frame. Join cabinets with sheetmetal screws.

6 Position and attach each additional cabinet. Clamp frames together, and drill counterbored pilot holes through side of face frame. Join cabinets with sheetmetal screws. Drill 3/16" pilot holes in hanging strips, and attach cabinet to studs with sheetmetal screws.

Join frameless cabinets with No. 8 gauge 1¼" wood screws and finish washers. Each pair of cabinets should be joined by at least four screws.

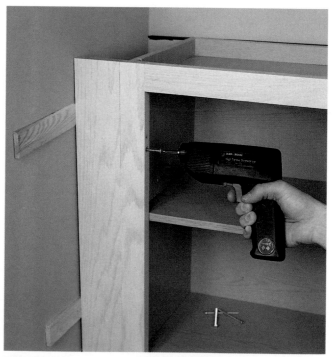

7 Fill small spaces between a cabinet and a wall or appliance with a filler strip. Cut filler to fit space, then wedge filler into place with wood shims. Drill counterbored pilot holes through side of cabinet face frame, and attach filler with sheetmetal screws.

8 Remove temporary ledger. Check cabinet run for plumb, and adjust if necessary by placing wood shims behind cabinet, near stud locations. Tighten wall screws completely. Cut off shims with utility knife.

9 Use trim moldings to cover any gaps between cabinets and walls. Stain moldings to match cabinet finish.

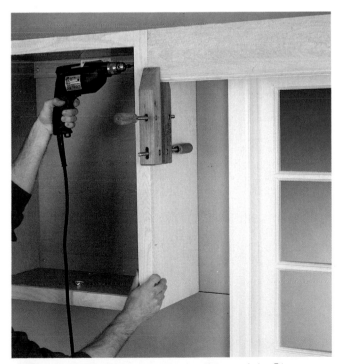

10 Attach decorative valance above sink. Clamp valance to edge of cabinet frames, and drill counterbored pilot holes through cabinet frames into end of valance. Attach with sheetmetal screws.

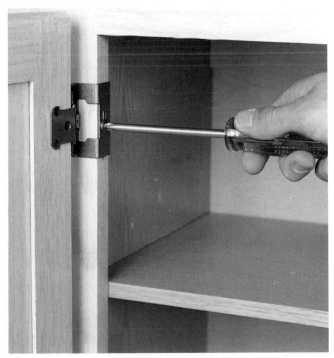

11 Install the cabinet doors. If necessary, adjust the hinges so that the doors are straight and plumb.

How to Install Base Cabinets

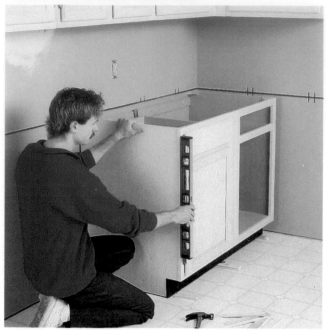

1 Begin installation with corner cabinet. Position cabinet so that top is flush with reference line. Make sure cabinet is plumb and level. If necessary, adjust by driving wood shims under cabinet base. Be careful not to damage flooring. Drill ³⁄₁₆" pilot holes through hanging strip into wall studs. Attach cabinets loosely to wall with sheetmetal screws.

2 Attach filler strip to adjoining cabinet, if necessary (page 135). Clamp filler in place, and drill counterbored pilot holes through side of face frame. Attach filler with sheetmetal screws.

3 Clamp adjoining cabinet to corner cabinet. Make sure cabinet is plumb, then drill counterbored pilot holes through corner-cabinet face frame into filler strip (page 136, step 5). Join cabinets with sheetmetal screws. Drill ³⁄₁₆" pilot holes through hanging strips into wall studs. Attach cabinets loosely with sheet-metal screws.

4 Use a jig saw to cut any cabinet openings needed for plumbing, wiring, or heating ducts.

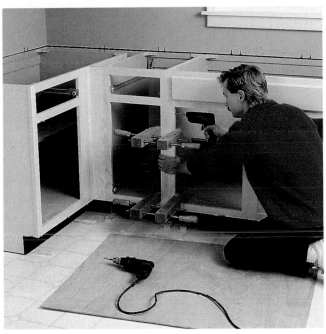

5 Position and attach additional cabinets, making sure frames are aligned. Clamp cabinets together, then drill counterbored pilot holes through side of face frame. Join cabinets with sheetmetal screws. Frameless cabinets are joined with No. 8 gauge 1¼" wood screws and finish washers (page 136).

6 Make sure all cabinets are level. If necessary, adjust by driving wood shims underneath cabinets. Place wood shims behind cabinets near stud locations wherever there is a gap. Tighten wall screws. Cut off shims with utility knife.

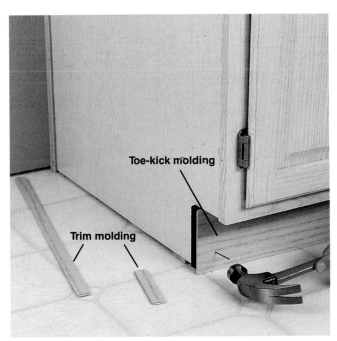

Toe-kick molding

Trim molding

7 Use trim moldings to cover gaps between the cabinets and the wall or floor. Toe-kick area is often covered with a strip of hardwood finished to match the cabinets.

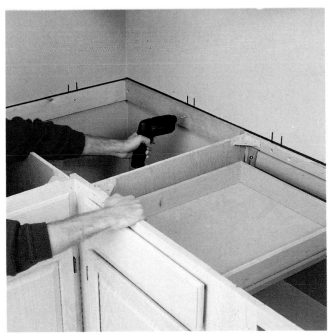

8 If corner has void area not covered by cabinets, screw 1 × 3 cleats to wall, flush with reference line. Cleats will help support countertop.

How to Install a Ceiling-hung Cabinet to Joists

1 Cut a cardboard template to same size as top of wall cabinet. Use template to outline position of cabinet on ceiling. Mark position of the cabinet face frame on the outline.

2 Locate joists with stud finder. If joists run parallel to cabinet, install blocking between joists to hang cabinet (below). Measure joist positions and mark cabinet frame to indicate where to drive screws.

3 Have one or more helpers position cabinet against ceiling. Drill ³⁄₁₆" pilot holes through top rails into ceiling joists. Attach cabinets with 4" wood screws and finish washers.

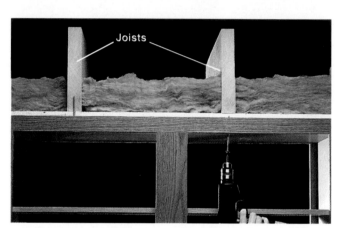

Shown in cutaway: Cabinet is attached to joists with wood screws and finish washers.

How to Attach a Ceiling-hung Cabinet to Blocking (joists must be accessible)

1 Drill reference holes through the ceiling at each corner of cabinet outline. From above ceiling, install 2 × 4 blocks between joists. Blocking can be toenailed, or end-nailed through joists.

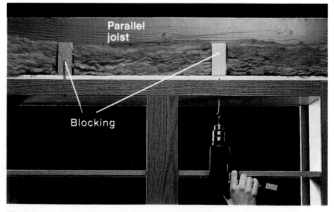

2 Measure distance between each block and the drilled reference holes. Mark cabinet frame to indicate where to drive anchoring screws. Drill pilot holes and attach cabinet to blocking with 4" wood screws and finish washers, as shown in cutaway (above).

140

How to Install a Base Island Cabinet

1 Set the base cabinet in the correct position, and lightly trace the cabinet outline on the flooring. Remove cabinet.

2 Attach L-shaped 2 × 4 cleats to floor at opposite corners of cabinet outline. Allow for thickness of cabinet walls by positioning cleats ¾" inside cabinet outline. Attach cleat to floor with 3" wallboard screws.

3 Lower the base cabinet over the cleats. Check cabinet for level, and shim under the base if necessary.

4 Attach the cabinet to the floor cleats using 6d finish nails. Drill pilot holes for nails, and recess nail heads with a nail set.

Plumbing & Appliances

Make final connections for faucets, drains, and appliances after an electrician or plumber has finished the rough work. A licensed plumber or electrician will make sure the job conforms to local codes.

Where codes allow, have the electrician install plug-in outlets for all the major appliances. This makes it easy to disconnect the appliances for servicing.

If a remodeling job requires new plumbing and wiring, the work should be completed in the early stage of the project, before new flooring, cabinets, or appliances are installed.

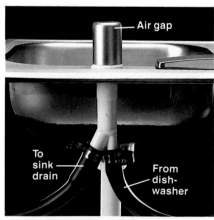

Dishwasher drain hose is looped up through an air gap device attached to the sink or countertop. Air gap is a safety feature that prevents a plugged sink drain from backing up into the dishwasher.

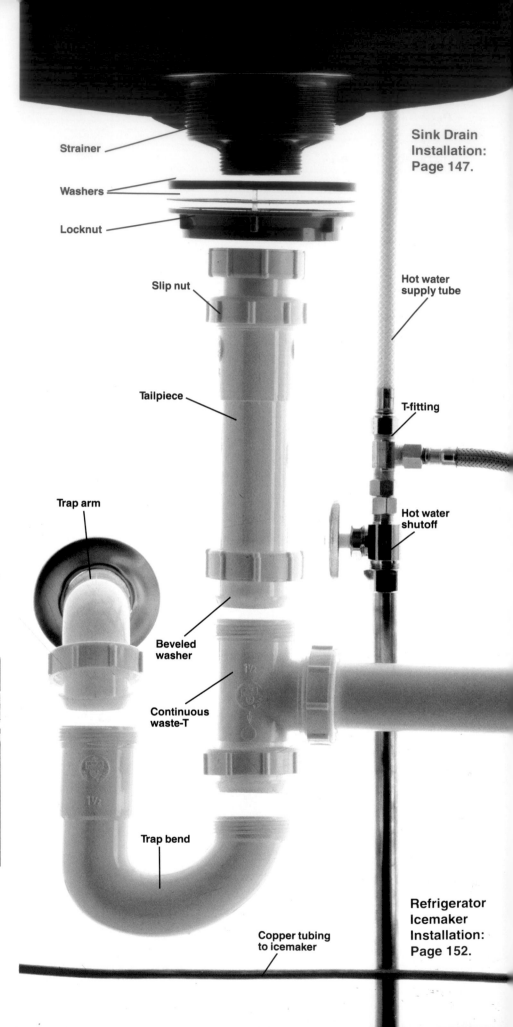

Sink Drain Installation: Page 147.

Strainer

Washers

Locknut

Slip nut

Hot water supply tube

Tailpiece

T-fitting

Trap arm

Hot water shutoff

Beveled washer

Continuous waste-T

Trap bend

Copper tubing to icemaker

Refrigerator Icemaker Installation: Page 152.

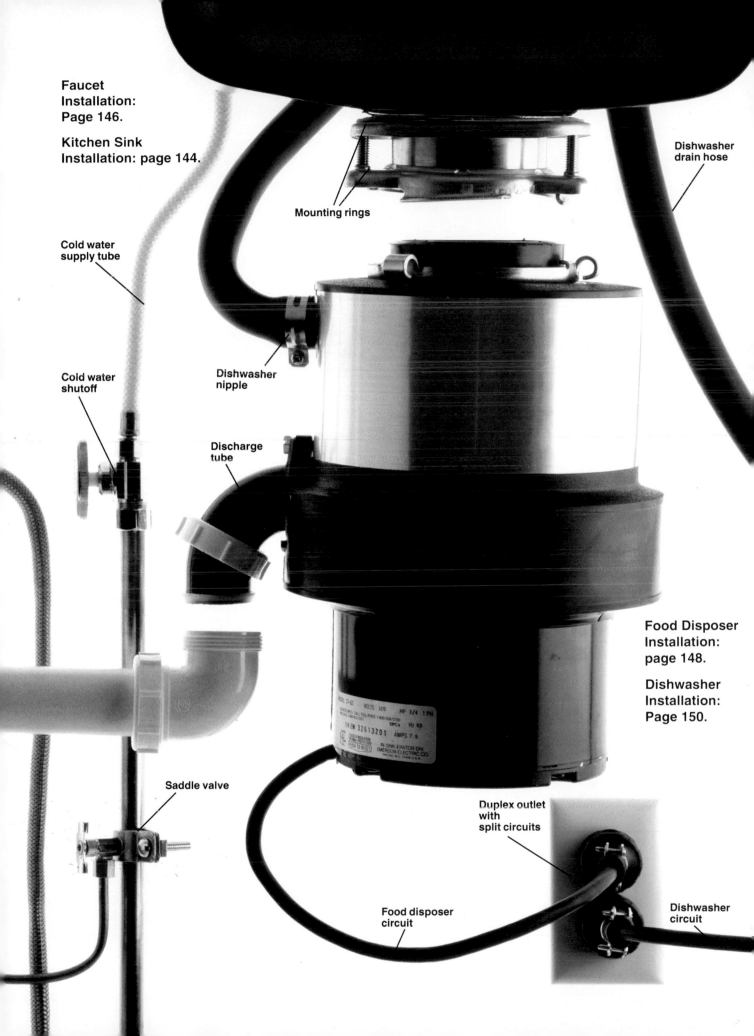

Faucet
Installation:
Page 146.

Kitchen Sink
Installation: page 144.

Mounting rings

Dishwasher
drain hose

Cold water
supply tube

Dishwasher
nipple

Cold water
shutoff

Discharge
tube

Food Disposer
Installation:
page 148.

Dishwasher
Installation:
Page 150.

Saddle valve

Duplex outlet
with
split circuits

Food disposer
circuit

Dishwasher
circuit

Installing a Kitchen Sink

Kitchen sinks for do-it-yourself installation are made from cast iron coated with enamel, stainless steel, or enameled steel.

Cast-iron sinks are heavy, durable, and relatively easy to install. Most cast-iron sinks are frameless, requiring no mounting hardware.

Stainless steel and enameled steel sinks weigh less than cast iron. They may require a metal frame and mounting brackets. A good stainless steel sink is made of heavy 18- or 20-gauge nickel steel, which holds up well under use. Lighter steel (designated by numbers higher than 20) dents easily.

Some premium-quality sinks are made from solid-surface material or porcelain, and are usually installed by professionals.

When choosing a sink, make sure the predrilled openings will fit your faucet. To make the countertop cutout for a kitchen sink installation, see page 69.

Specialty Tools & Supplies for plumbing & appliance installation include: plumber's putty (A), hacksaw (B), silicone caulk (C), tubing cutter (D), hole saw (E), channel-type pliers (F), hose clamps (G), combination tool (H).

Everything You Need:

Basic Hand Tools (page 62): caulk gun, screwdriver.

Basic Materials: sink, sink frame, mounting clips.

Specialty Tools & Supplies: photo, left.

How to Install a Frameless Sink

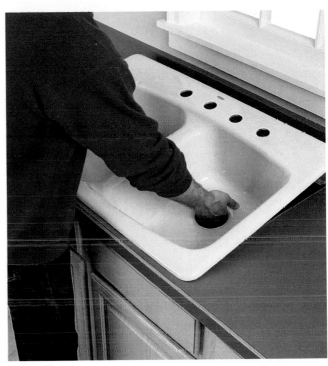

1 After making countertop cutout, lay the sink upside down. Apply a ¼" bead of silicone caulk or plumber's putty around the underside of sink flange.

2 Position front of sink in countertop cutout, by holding it from the drain openings. Carefully lower the sink into position. Press down to create a tight seal, then wipe away excess caulk.

How to Install a Framed Sink

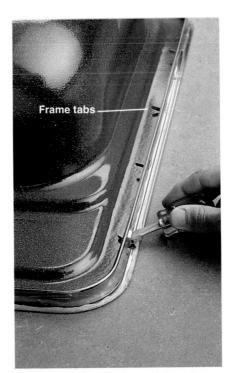

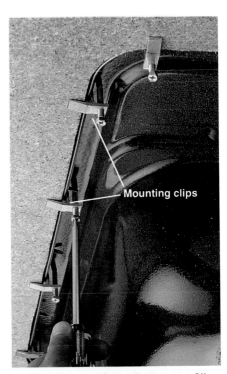

1 Turn the sink frame upside down. Apply a ¼" bead of silicone caulk or plumber's putty around both sides of the vertical flange.

2 Set the sink upside down inside the frame. Bend frame tabs to hold the sink. Carefully set the sink into the cutout opening, and press down to create a tight seal.

3 Hook mounting clips every 6" to 8" inches around the frame from underneath countertop. Tighten mounting screws. Wipe away excess caulk from the frame.

Installing a Faucet & Drain

Most new kitchen faucets feature single-handle control levers and washerless designs. They rarely require maintenance. More expensive designer styles offer added features, like colorful enameled finishes, detachable spray nozzles, or even digital temperature readouts.

Connect the faucet to hot and cold water lines with easy-to-install flexible supply tubes made from vinyl or braided steel.

Where local codes allow, use plastic piping for drain hookups. Plastic is inexpensive and easy to install.

A wide selection of extensions and angle fittings let you easily plumb any sink configuration. Manufacturers offer kits that contain all the fittings needed for attaching a food disposer or dishwasher to the sink drain system.

Everything You Need:

Basic Materials: faucet, flexible vinyl or braided steel supply tubes, drain components.

Specialty Tools & Supplies: photo, page 144.

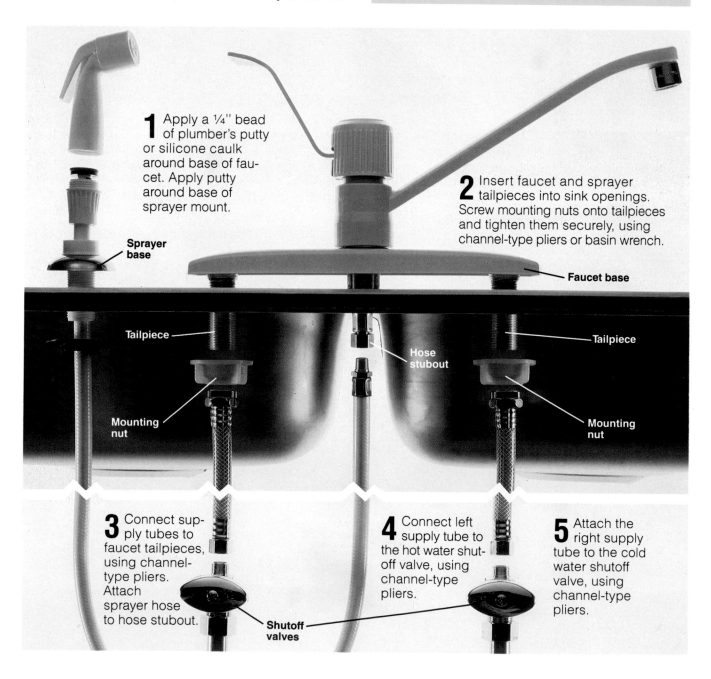

1 Apply a ¼" bead of plumber's putty or silicone caulk around base of faucet. Apply putty around base of sprayer mount.

Sprayer base

2 Insert faucet and sprayer tailpieces into sink openings. Screw mounting nuts onto tailpieces and tighten them securely, using channel-type pliers or basin wrench.

Faucet base

Tailpiece

Hose stubout

Tailpiece

Mounting nut

Mounting nut

3 Connect supply tubes to faucet tailpieces, using channel-type pliers. Attach sprayer hose to hose stubout.

Shutoff valves

4 Connect left supply tube to the hot water shut-off valve, using channel-type pliers.

5 Attach the right supply tube to the cold water shutoff valve, using channel-type pliers.

How to Attach Drain Lines

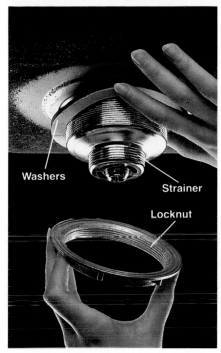

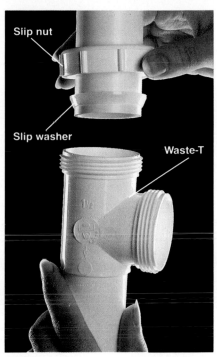

1 Install sink strainer in each sink drain opening. Apply ¼" bead of plumber's putty around bottom of flange. Insert strainer into drain opening. Place rubber and fiber washers over neck of strainer. Screw locknut onto neck and tighten with channel-type pliers.

2 Attach tailpiece to strainer. Place insert washer in flared end of tailpiece, then attach tailpiece by screwing a slip nut onto sink strainer. If necessary, tailpiece can be cut to fit with a hacksaw.

3 On sinks with two basins, use a continuous waste-T-fitting to join the tailpieces (pages 142 to 143). Attach the fitting with slip washers and nuts. Beveled side of washers face threaded portion of pipes.

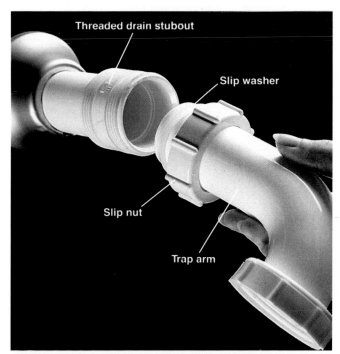

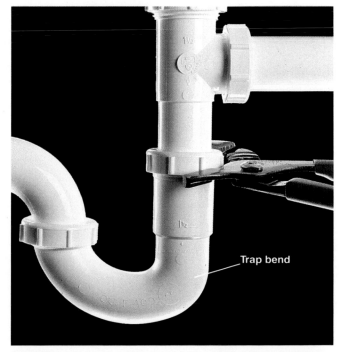

4 Attach the trap arm to the drain stubout, using a slip nut and washer. Beveled side of washer should face threaded drain stubout. If necessary, trap arm can be cut to fit with a hacksaw.

5 Attach trap bend to trap arm, using slip nuts and washers. Beveled side of washers should face trap bend. Tighten all nuts with channel-type pliers.

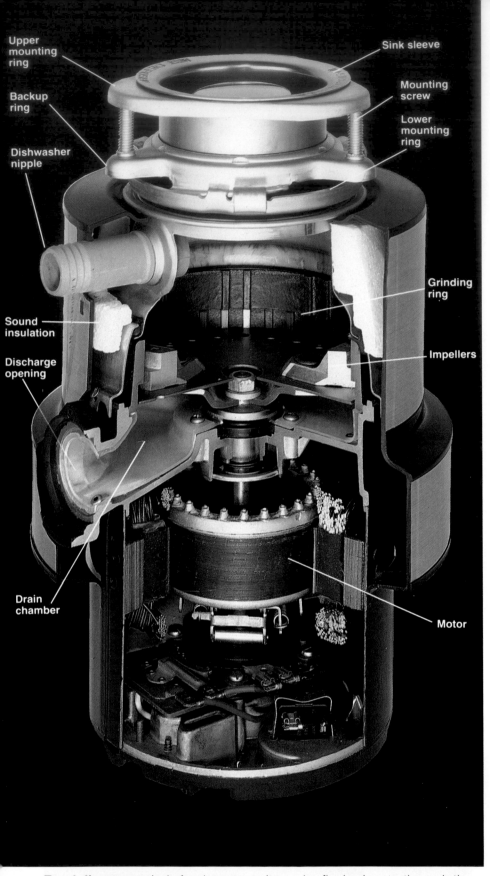

Upper mounting ring

Backup ring

Dishwasher nipple

Sound insulation

Discharge opening

Drain chamber

Sink sleeve

Mounting screw

Lower mounting ring

Grinding ring

Impellers

Motor

Food disposer grinds food waste so it can be flushed away through the sink drain system. A quality disposer has a ½-horsepower, self-reversing motor that will not jam. Other features to look for include foam sound insulation, a cast-iron grinding ring, and overload protection that allows the motor to be reset if it overheats. Better food disposers have a 5-year manufacturer's warranty.

Installing a Food Disposer

Choose a food disposer with a motor rated at ½ horsepower or more. Look for a self-reversing feature that prevents the disposer from jamming. Better models carry a manufacturer's warranty of up to five years.

Local plumbing codes may require that a disposer be plugged into a grounded outlet controlled by a switch above the sink.

Everything You Need:

Basic Hand Tools (page 62): screwdriver.

Basic Materials: 12-gauge appliance cord with grounded plug, wire nuts.

Specialty Tools & Supplies: photo, page 144.

How to Install a Food Disposer

1 Remove plate on bottom of disposer. Use combination tool to strip about ½" of insulation from each wire in appliance cord. Connect white wires, using a wire nut. Connect black wires. Attach green insulated wire to green ground screw. Gently push wires into opening. Replace bottom plate.

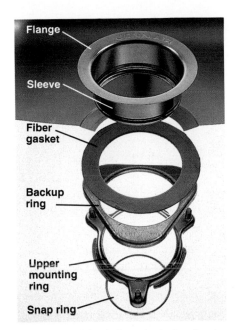

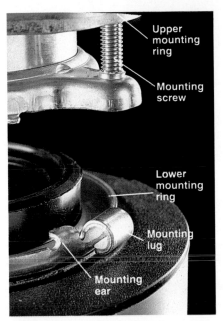

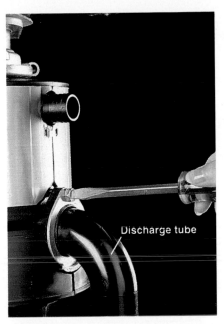

2 Apply ¼-inch bead of plumber's putty under the flange of the disposer sink sleeve. Insert sleeve in drain opening, and slip the fiber gasket and the backup ring onto the sleeve. Place upper mounting ring on sleeve and slide snap ring into groove.

3 Tighten the three mounting screws. Hold disposer against upper mounting ring so that the mounting lugs on the lower mounting ring are directly under the mounting screws. Turn the lower mounting ring clockwise until the disposer is supported by the mounting assembly.

4 Attach the discharge tube to the discharge opening on the side of the disposer, using the rubber washer and metal flange.

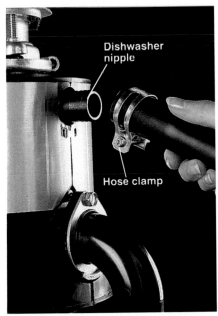

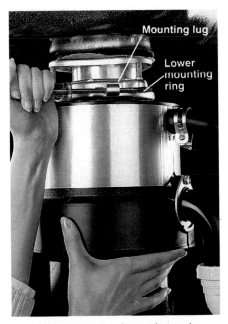

5 If dishwasher will be attached, knock out the plug in the dishwasher nipple, using a screwdriver. Attach the dishwasher drain hose to nipple with hose clamp.

6 Attach the discharge tube to continuous waste pipe with slip washer and nut. If discharge tube is too long, cut it with a hacksaw or tubing cutter.

7 Lock disposer into place. Insert a screwdriver or disposer wrench into a mounting lug on the lower mounting ring, and turn clockwise until the mounting ears are locked. Tighten all drain slip nuts with channel-type pliers.

Installing a Dishwasher

A dishwasher requires a hot water supply connection, a drain connection, and an electrical hookup. These connections are easiest to make when the dishwasher is located next to the sink.

Hot water reaches the dishwasher through a supply tube. With a multiple-outlet shutoff valve or brass T-fitting on the hot water pipe, you can control water to the sink and dishwasher with the same valve.

For safety, loop the dishwasher drain hose up through an air gap mounted on the sink or countertop. An air gap prevents a clogged drain from backing up into the dishwasher.

A dishwasher requires its own 20-amp electrical circuit. For convenience, have this circuit wired into one-half of a split duplex receptacle. The other half of the receptacle powers the food disposer.

Everything You Need:

Basic Hand Tools (page 62): screwdriver, utility knife.

Basic Power Tools (page 63): drill with 2" hole saw.

Basic Materials: air gap, drain hose, waste-T tailpiece, braided steel supply tube, rubber connector for food disposer, brass L-fitting, 12-gauge appliance power cord.

Specialty Tools & Supplies: photo, page 144.

How to Install a Dishwasher

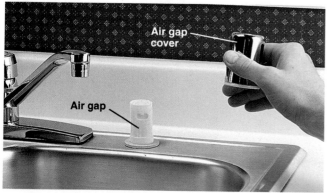

1 Mount air gap, using one of the predrilled sink openings. Or, bore a hole in the countertop with a drill and hole saw. Attach the air gap by tightening mounting nut over the tailpiece with channel-type pliers.

2 Cut openings in side of sink base cabinet for electrical and plumbing lines, using a drill and hole saw. Dishwasher instructions specify size and location of openings. Slide dishwasher into place, feeding rubber drain hose through hole in cabinet. Level the dishwasher (page 152).

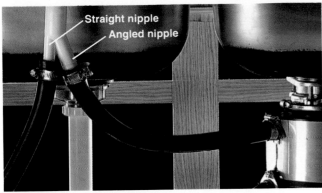

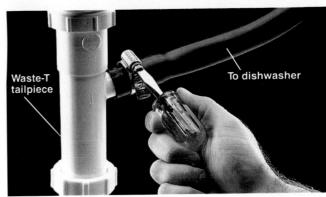

3 Attach the dishwasher drain hose to the smaller, straight nipple on the air gap, using a hose clamp. If hose is too long, cut to correct length with a utility knife. Cut another length of rubber hose to reach from the larger, angled nipple to the food disposer. Attach hose to the air gap and to the nipple on disposer with hose clamps.

On sinks without food disposer, attach a special waste-T sink tailpiece to sink strainer. Attach the drain hose to the waste-T nipple with a hose clamp.

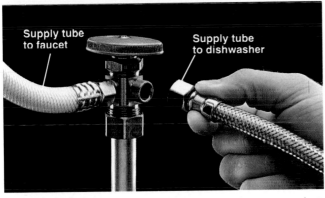

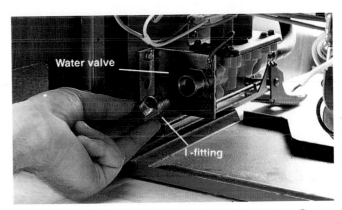

4 Connect dishwasher supply tube to hot water shut-off, using channel-type pliers. This connection is easiest with a multiple-outlet shutoff valve or a brass T-fitting (page 142).

5 Remove access panel on front of dishwasher. Connect a brass L-fitting to the threaded opening on the dishwasher water valve, and tighten with channel-type pliers.

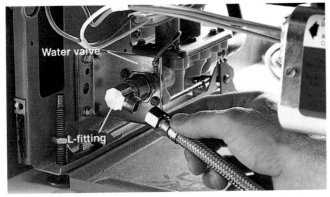

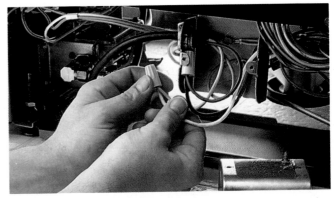

6 Run the braided steel supply tube from the hot water pipe to the dishwasher water valve. Attach supply tube to L-fitting, using channel-type pliers.

7 Remove cover on electrical box. Run power cord from outlet through to electrical box. Strip about ½" of insulation from each cord wire, using combination tool. Connect black wires, using a wire nut. Connect white wires. Connect green insulated wire to ground screw. Replace box cover and dishwasher access panel.

Installing Appliances

New appliances may require that electrical circuits, plumbing, or gas lines be updated by an electrician or plumber. Large electrical appliances each require a separate circuit. Gas lines should have accessible shutoff valves.

If electrical or plumbing improvements have been made, have a building inspector review the work before you connect the appliances.

Everything You Need:

Basic Materials: ¼" soft copper tubing, saddle valve, brass compression fittings.

Specialty Tools & Supplies: photo, page 144, appliance dolly.

How to Level Appliances

Level large appliances, like a refrigerator or dishwasher, by rotating the threaded front feet with channel-type pliers. On some appliances, you must remove an access panel to adjust the legs.

Move heavy appliances with a rented appliance dolly. Make sure appliances are strapped tightly to dolly. To position large appliances, you may need a helper.

How to Connect Refrigerator Icemaker

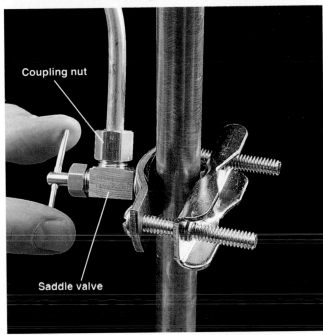

1 Shut off water at main shutoff valve. Attach a ¼"
saddle valve to cold water pipe. Connect ¼" soft
copper tubing to saddle valve with compression ring
and coupling nut. Closing spigot fully causes spike
inside valve to puncture water pipe.

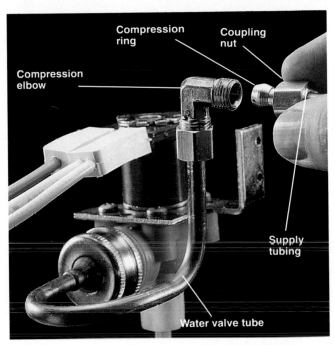

2 Run copper tubing to refrigerator. Connect water
supply tube to the water valve tube, using a ¼"
compression elbow. Slide coupling nuts and compression rings over tubes, and insert tubes into elbow.
Tighten coupling nuts with channel-type pliers.

How to Make Electrical Connections

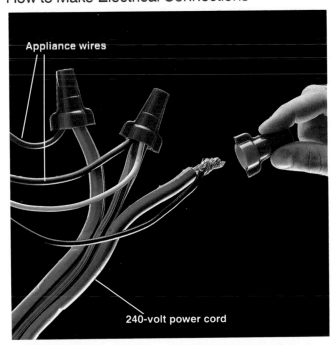

Use wire nuts to connect power cord to appliance
wires. Power cord for a 240-volt appliance has three
leads. Turn power off. Strip about ⅝" of insulation from
each lead. Attach the white appliance wire, and green
wire (if present), to the middle lead on power cord,
using a large wire nut. Attach red and black appliance
wires to the outside leads on power cord.

How to Connect Gas Lines

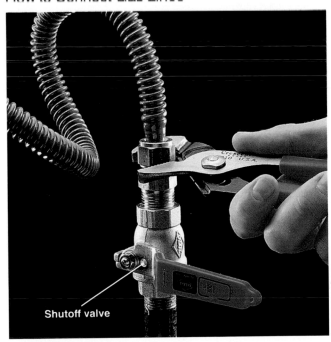

Connect flexible gas tubing to shutoff valve and to
appliance, using channel-type pliers. Follow local
code requirements for gas connections.

153

Installing a Vent Hood

A vent hood eliminates heat, moisture, and cooking vapors from your kitchen. It has an electric fan unit with one or more filters, and a system of metal ducts to vent air to the outdoors. A ducted vent hood is more efficient than a ductless model, which filters and recirculates air without removing it.

Metal ducts for a vent hood can be round or rectangular. Elbows and transition fittings are available for both types of ducts. These fittings let you vent around corners, or join duct components that differ in shape or size.

Wall-mounted vent hood (shown in cutaway) is installed between wall cabinets. Fan unit is fastened to a metal liner that is anchored to cabinets. Duct and elbow fitting exhaust cooking vapors to the outdoors through a wall cap. Vent fan and duct are covered by wood or laminate panels that match cabinet finish.

Everything You Need:

Basic Hand Tools (page 62): tape measure, screwdrivers, hammer, eye protection, pencil.

Basic Power Tools (page 63): drill.

Basic Materials: duct sections, duct elbow, duct cap, vent hood, 1½" sheetmetal screws, 1¼" wallboard screws.

Specialty Tools & Supplies: photo, below.

Specialty tools & supplies include: reciprocating saw with coarse wood-cutting blade (A), silicone caulk (B), duct tape (C), wire nuts (D), ⅛" twist bit (E), No. 9 counterbore drill bit (F), ¾" sheetmetal screws (G), 2½" sheetmetal screws (H), combination tool (I), masonry chisel (J), 2" masonry nails (K), metal snips (L), masonry drill bit (M), ball peen hammer (N).

154

How to Install a Wall-mounted Vent Hood

1 Attach ¾" × 4" × 12" wooden cleats to sides of the cabinets with 1¼" wallboard screws. Follow manufacturer's directions for proper distance from cooking surface.

2 Position the hood liner between the cleats and attach with ¾" sheetmetal screws.

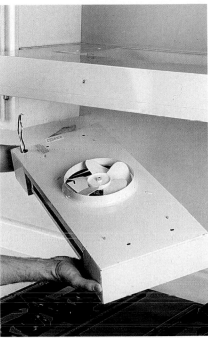

3 Remove cover panels for light, fan, and electrical compartments on fan unit, as directed by manufacturer. Position fan unit inside liner and fasten by attaching nuts to mounting bolts inside light compartments.

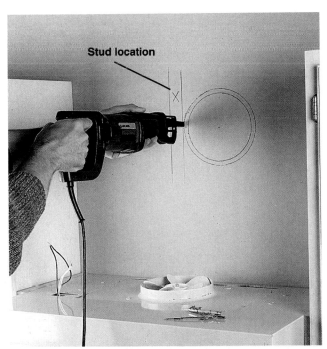

4 Locate studs in wall where duct will pass, using a stud finder. Mark hole location. Hole should be ½" larger that diameter of duct. Complete cutout with a reciprocating saw or jig saw. Remove any wall insulation. Drill a pilot hole through outside wall.

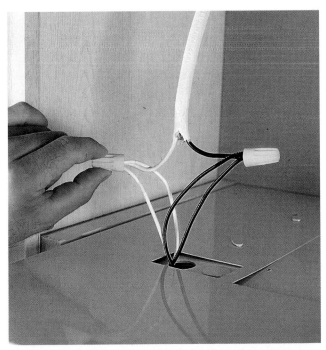

5 Strip about ½" of plastic insulation from each wire in the circuit cable, using combination tool. Connect the black wires, using a wire nut. Connect the white wires. Gently push the wires into the electrical box. Replace the coverpanels on the light and fan compartments.

(continued next page)

6 Make duct cutout on exterior wall. On masonry, drill a series of holes around outline of cutout. Remove waste with a masonry chisel and ball peen hammer. On wood siding, make cutout with a reciprocating saw.

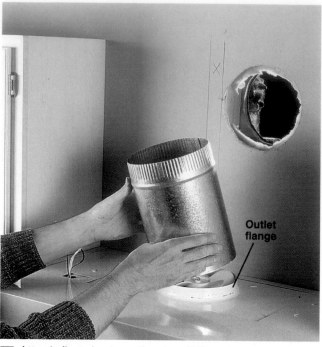

7 Attach first duct section by sliding the smooth end over the outlet flange on the vent hood. Cut duct sections to length with metal snips.

Outlet flange

8 Drill three or four pilot holes around joint through both layers of metal, using ⅛" twist bit. Attach duct with ¾" sheetmetal screws. Seal joint with duct tape.

9 Join additional duct sections by sliding smooth end over corrugated end of preceding section. Use an adjustable elbow to change directions in duct run. Secure all joints with sheetmetal screws and duct tape.

10 Install duct cap on exterior wall. Apply a thick bead of silicone caulk to cap flange. Slide cap over end of duct.

11 Attach cap to wall with 2'' masonry nails, or 1½'' sheetmetal screws (on wood siding). Wipe away excess caulk.

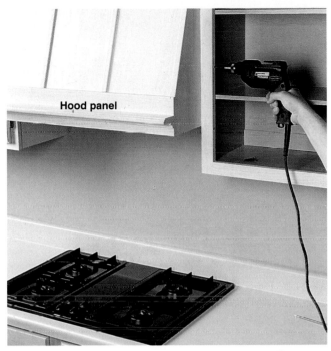

12 Slide the decorative hood panel into place between the wall cabinets. Drill pilot holes through the cabinet face frame with a counterbore bit. Attach the hood panel to the cabinets with 2½'' sheetmetal screws.

Vent Hood Variations

Downdraft cooktop has a built-in blower unit that vents through the back or the bottom of a base cabinet. A downdraft cooktop is a good choice for a kitchen island or peninsula.

Cabinet-mounted vent hood is attached to the bottom of a short, 12'' to 18'' tall wall cabinet. Metal ducts run inside this wall cabinet.

Index